West African History

A Captivating Guide to the History of West Africa and the Yoruba People

Free Bonus from Captivating History (Available for a Limited time)

Hi History Lovers!

Now you have a chance to join our exclusive history list so you can get your first history ebook for free as well as discounts and a potential to get more history books for free! Simply visit the link below to join.

Captivatinghistory.com/ebook

Also, make sure to follow us on Facebook, Twitter and Youtube by searching for Captivating History.

Table of Contents

Part 1: The Yoruba People

A Captivating Guide to the History of the Yorubas and Yoruba Mythology

Introduction

The Yoruba People: A Captivating Guide to the History of the Yorubas and Yoruba Mythology is not just a collection of events. It is a detailed compilation of the culture, history, practices, and legends that form the experiences of the Yoruba people. This book will serve as an excellent foundation to better understand how the ethos of the ancient Yorubas shaped the lives of the present Yoruba people.

According to a study carried out at the University of Florida, there are twenty-five million Yoruba people globally. Some scholars argue that there are over fifty million Yoruba people, with Nigeria alone having an estimated population of about forty million. The disparity in these figures may be due to the fact that many Yoruba people have migrated from West Africa and now live in almost every country all over the world. But who exactly are the Yoruba people? Where did they originate? What language do they speak, and where can they be found? You can expect to find the answers to all of these questions and more in this book.

Read how the lifestyle of the Yoruba people changed but still manages to contain elements of their forefathers. Let this book take you on a journey that spans over fifteen centuries!

Let's get started.

Chapter 1 – Yoruba: The Origins

A Brief Introduction to the Yoruba People

To start with, the word Yoruba, pronounced "yaw-roo-buh," is used to describe both a language and an ethnic group. Therefore, it is difficult to speak about the Yoruba people without discussing the language itself. The Yoruba people can be primarily found in Nigeria, Benin, and Togo, as they originated from these countries. As mentioned earlier, due to their high rate of emigration, they can also be found in other places and have high residency rates in countries like Ghana, the United States, the United Kingdom, Italy, and Canada.

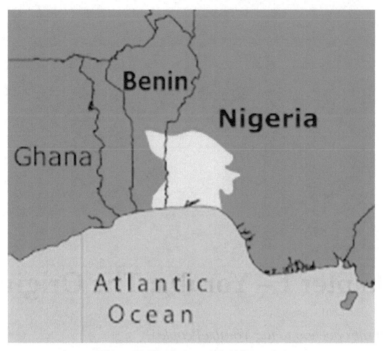

Where the Yoruba people initially settled

Interestingly, the term Yoruba was not always used for the Yoruba-speaking people. In fact, it didn't officially come into use until the 19th century. The Hausa people originally used the word Yoruba to reference the Oyo people of Nigeria. The Hausas, who are well known for their nomadic habits, popularized the name during their travels all over West Africa.

Prior to Yoruba being used as the standardized term to describe the entire ethnic group, they were known by different names in different regions. One of the many names ascribed to them is Aku, which was taken from the first word in their greetings—*E ku aaro*, meaning "good morning," and *E ku ale*, meaning "good night."

Another term used for the Yoruba people is Okun, which is a slight variation of *Aku*, and *Anago* or *Nago*, which was derived from the Yoruba group in the Republic of Benin. Lucumi, which was derived from *o luku mi*, meaning "my friend," was another term used to describe the Yorubas in Cuba and some other Spanish-speaking countries.

Prior to these terms, the Yorubas described themselves as *omo Oduduwa*, meaning "the children of Oduduwa," referencing the man who is believed to be the founding father of the Yorubas. They also describe themselves as *omo Karo-oojiire*, meaning "the people who ask good morning, did you wake up well?" The reason for this term is due to the well-practiced act of greeting others in the Yoruba culture. The Yorubas have a specific greeting for any situation. For example, *E ku ewa o* is used to salute hairstylists while they are performing a service, and *E ku ewu omo o* is used to praise mothers who have just given birth.

The Yoruba language is said to have developed out of the Volt-Niger branch of the Niger-Congo group of languages. It is classified among the Edekiri languages, which include the Yoruba languages, the Ede dialect, and Itsekiri. These languages are spoken across Togo, Nigeria, and Benin. Some believe that the Yoruba language has over forty million speakers in Nigeria. It is the most spoken African language outside of Africa.

For those interested in linguistics, the Yoruba language can be further divided into five dialects: Southeast, Northeast, Southwest, Northwest, and Central. There are many variations existing within these five major dialects, with a thin line differentiating them from one another. For instance, the Northwest Yoruba dialect includes sub-dialects such as Oyo, Lagos, Ibadan, Egba, and Yewa, while the Northeast dialect consists of the sub-dialects of Abunu, Yagba, and Ijumu. Interestingly, the Yoruba language spoken in these five major regions differs greatly, and it may be difficult for some of these people to understand each other.

Accounts of Creation

The Yoruba culture is primarily oral, which means history was passed down through stories, legends, and folklore. In the Yoruba culture, the families responsible for telling the stories had to be appointed by the king, and the role of historian was inherited by the family member who received the most training or knew the most stories. As to be expected, the stories vary.

Just as the scientific world has a widely accepted theory of creation (the Big Bang), the Yorubas have their own account of creation. Although, it is probably more accurate to say accounts since there is more than one accepted version. The first and most widely popular account of creation is told as follows.

In the beginning, the whole universe was made up of the sky above and the water below. The entire surface of the earth was covered in water. Olodumare, the king of the heavens or the supreme being, sent down some divine beings to establish life on earth. While preparing for this journey, Olodumare gave them one chicken, a calabash (a type of gourd) containing sand, and one palm nut. These heavenly beings descended to earth by a chain and landed on the spot known as Ife, which is regarded as the heart of Yorubaland. The heavenly beings poured the sand on the surface of the water and placed the chicken on it. As the chicken began to scratch the sand with its claws, the sand began to spread until it formed the islands and continents of the world.

Another account of this story states that the heavenly beings went with a chameleon, and as the fowl spread the sand over the earth, the chameleon determined if the land was dry and solid enough. It is also believed that the areas still covered with water are those places not touched by the sand. The heavenly beings planted the palm nut, and it grew into the plants we have today. The human race was said to have descended from the heavenly beings where it all started, in Ile-Ife. This creation account implies that the Yorubas were the first humans and that other humans and civilizations originated from Nigeria.

Another notable creation story similar to the one above states that when Oduduwa, popularly known as the Father of Yorubaland, was sent to create humankind, he was given a chicken and a bag of sand. As he descended down a long chain, he lost his grip on the chicken. While attempting to catch the falling chicken, he lost his grip on the bag of sand. The sand plummeted, and by the time Oduduwa recovered, the sand had already formed a mound, with the chicken seated atop it. The sand started expanding, and he exclaimed, "Ile n'fe!" meaning "The land is expanding!"

Another slightly different creation account states that Olodumare sent a group of heavenly beings on an expedition. According to this account, Olodumare made Obatala the leader of this expedition, but along the way, Obatala got drunk and fell into a drunken stupor. Due to this, Oduduwa had to take over the expedition, and he subsequently completed the mission, thus making him the father of the Yoruba people and all the people of the world.

Another version says that the Yorubas migrated from Mecca and were descended from Lamurudu, one of the kings of Mecca. One of Lamurudu's offspring is Oduduwa, who is the ancestor of the Yoruba people. However, this version did not state the period when Lamurudu was in power, but it talks about the revolution among his descendants and their dispersion. During this period, the crown prince Oduduwa wanted to change the state religion to idolatry, so he turned the mosque into a temple for idol worship. He had a chief priest called Asara, who himself was an idol-maker. Asara had a son named Braima, who, as a child, detested his father's profession. He grew up to become a follower of Muhammad (the founder of Islam). While he helped his father sell some of the carved images, he wasn't a willing participant.

The town frequently went on three-day hunting expeditions to celebrate the gods. Braima used one of these occasions to destroy the gods in the temple since those that might oppose him were out of town. When the expedition party returned and discovered what Braima had done, he was ordered to be burned alive. This led to a war between the followers of the gods and the Muslims. The Muslims won the war, and Lamurudu was killed. His children and their sympathizers were driven out of Mecca. Oduduwa and his children escaped with two idols, and they journeyed eastward for ninety days until they reached Ife, where they settled. (Ife is another name for the aforementioned Ile-Ife.)

Considering their manners and customs, it is undeniable that the Yorubas migrated from the east; however, it is highly disputable that they originated from the Arabian region. Mecca has no record of them in its history books, and such an important event would not have gone unnoticed. However, these accounts sometimes do have a grain of truth in them, so it is possible that more may be uncovered as time passes.

After Oduduwa settled in Ife, he gave birth to a son named Okanbi. Okanbi had seven children who would later establish the different kingdoms that make up some of the Yoruba lands today. The names of the princes and princesses are Owu, Orangun, Popo, Sabe, Ketu, Oyo, and Benin. Oduduwa also had a grandson named Oranyan, who would later establish one of the biggest Yoruba empires.

Despite all of these varying creation accounts, there is no doubt that the Yorubas regard Oduduwa as their founding and spiritual father.

Origins of the Tribes

The Yoruba might be one large ethnic group, but there are many tribes within the culture that, in one way or another, can trace their origin to Oduduwa and the city of Ile-Ife. As said earlier, most of the major tribes sprang from Oduduwa's grandchildren. All of the other minor tribes originated from one of these seven tribes: Ketu, Owu, Sabe, Orangun, Ila,

Popo, and Benin. When Oduduwa migrated from the east, there is a possibility that the eastern region contained natives who were conquered and absorbed into the culture. The Yoruba culture established and extended their kingdom as far as Ashanti, Ghana, because Oranyan and his brother were able to push their conquest in every direction.

Oyo

Oranyan is known as the founder of the Oyo Empire. He was the youngest among the seven grandchildren of Oduduwa. Before he departed from Ife, Oranyan was already a distinguished and brave warrior. This is probably one of the reasons why he became successful in his conquests. According to one account, Oranyan agreed with his brother to attack a northern kingdom that had insulted his grandfather. Another version of the event said Oranyan left on an expedition to Mecca to avenge the death of his great-grandfather.

On the way, the two brothers quarreled and split up, going their separate ways. Oranyan wandered south to Bussa, where a chief there extended his hospitality. After explaining his predicament to the chief, Oranyan was given a charmed snake. As instructed, Oranyan followed the snake for seven days until it arrived at a spot and vanished into the ground. There, Oranyan established the Oyo Empire.

While the city was still under construction, they were constantly attacked by the Bariba of Borgu, who wanted to dominate the new city. At this point, the warrior Ajagunla (also known as Orangun, one of the legendary grandsons of Oduduwa) stepped in and helped the newly founded city win the war. Not long after this, Oranyan had a son named Ajuwon Ajaka. Much later, he gave birth to another son known as Shango.

Oranyan became the first Oba (ruler) of the Oyo Empire, and Shango, known as the Thunder God, became the third king. The empire no longer exists today, though there is still a ruler over the city of Odo who claims ancestry to Oranyan. The current Alaafin (emperor) of Oyo is

Lamidi Olayiwola Adeyemi III.

Ijebu

The Ijebus have different accounts of their origin. One version states they are descended from a victim who had been offered for sacrifice by the king of Benin to the god of the ocean. However, another account claims that the Ijebus are descended from Obanta, who was offered as a human sacrifice by the king of Owu. After being left for dead, he revived and crawled into a bush, where he survived on fruit before later dabbling in farming.

It is worth noting that in both accounts, the founders were victims of human sacrifice. Another account claims that Obanta led people out of Ile-Ife to form Ijebu-Ode. He led them until he reached old age, at which point he was instructed by Ifa (the chief god and the god of divination) to leave and die outside of the town.

The kings of the Ijebus are known as Awujale, and the current Awujale of the Ijebu Kingdom is Sikiru Kayode Adetona.

Ondo

The killing of twins was a prevalent practice among the early Yoruba people. And somehow, this practice is what brought about the establishment of the Ondo Kingdom. One of the wives of the Oyo Empire birthed twins in an era when twins were considered an abomination. The Alaafin, Oluaso, was not happy about this and ordered them removed from the kingdom. The princess left with a number of friends and journeyed to the present site of Ondo, meaning "settler." One of the twins died at Epe, which was near Ondo. The other twin, Airo, would later become the Osemawe of Ondo. The current Osemawe is Dr. Victor A. Kiladejo.

Egba

The Egba people established their homeland in the Egba forest after migrating from Oyo. Most families in Egba can trace their ancestry to Oyo, hence the popular saying, "Egbas who do not have Oyo roots must be slaves." This means that if they could not trace their roots, they must have belonged to the early Egba people, who were conquered by the settlers.

Over the centuries, the Egba people evolved from small hamlets to villages and are now cities, which operate independently. The first Alake of Egbaland was Okukenu Sagbua, and the current one is Adedotun Aremu Gbadebo III.

Ekiti

The Ekiti people are among the original inhabitants of the country absorbed by Oduduwa when he migrated from Mecca. Ekiti means "mound," which is derived from the mountainous features of the area. The region has extensive vegetation and is well watered.

One account says the Ekiti people are descended from one of the offspring of Oduduwa. Olofin, one of Oduduwa's offspring, had sixteen children of his own. Olofin decided to venture from Ife in search of greener pastures. Olofin and his offspring journeyed until they reached flat terrain. Two of his children decided to stay behind while the rest of the family continued their journey until they reached a land with many hills. Thus, they named the place *Ile olokiti*, meaning the "land of hills." The Ekiti Kingdom was divided into several kingdoms over time. Today, Ekiti State is one of the states that comprises Nigeria.

Ijesha

The Ijesha have different origin stories because their founder was different from the present-day people. The first account relates to the earliest Yoruba people when they had just migrated from the east and subdued the natives. At this time, human sacrifices were common, and slaves were often used as the victims. Slaves were captured from a district called Obokun and treated like cattle to be sacrificed to the gods. This prompted the name *Ije orisa*, meaning "foods for the gods."

Another account says the present-day Ijesha hailed from Ekiti. According to the customs back then, they were to go on a three-month hunting expedition for their king every year. On one such expedition, they found a region with plenty of game and an agreeable climate. The native Ijesha (probably a remnant of the former sacrificial victim) was peaceful. However, these people were quickly subdued by the invaders. One of their chiefs was spared due to his kind and gentle nature. He quickly rose through the ranks and eventually became the second-in-command to the chiefs of the invaders. The current Oba of Ijeshaland is Oba Gabriel Adekunle Aromolaranfall.

Chapter 2 – The Development of the Early Yoruba Society

After the establishment of the early Yoruba kingdoms, the people began to advance in terms of civilization and structure. The Iron Age brought about a significant transformation, as it would stimulate a great advancement of culture. The Iron Age first came to Nigeria in early 700 BCE. According to archaeologists, the knowledge of ironworking might have arrived in West Africa through pot production.

The ironmaking process is a dangerous occupation that requires the use of a high amount of heat. Due to this, most iron-smelting centers were located far from residential areas, usually in the forest, where iron-bearing rock clay is readily available. This iron-bearing rock clay is heated to remove the iron from its ore, where it is cooled and sold to the blacksmith as iron ingots. The blacksmiths used the ingot to fabricate tools.

In the Yoruba culture, iron smelting and the fabrication of tools from iron is overseen by one of their deities known as Ogun (also known as

Alakaaiye, meaning "the wielder of arms of working people"). Ogun is believed to be the god of iron and the patron of all working men. Iron-smelting workshops served as shrines to this deity, and sacrifices were rendered to the deity in the workshop. Blacksmiths were not the only ones that worshiped Ogun; it is believed that people using any form of metal in their daily activities (sculptors, farmers, woodworkers, hunters, etc.) offered sacrifices to this deity for good luck.

The discovery of iron was the second greatest discovery in West Africa after the discovery of agriculture. The Iron Age impacted the Yoruba culture positively, especially as it helped in the improvement of farming tools. Their first fabricated tools were crude at first but improved considerably with time. The improved tools made it possible to clear a large portion of land and dig and till the land for agricultural purposes. With more refined tools, more land became accessible for agriculture. Early Yoruba farmers learned quite early on the importance of leaving the ground fallow to retain soil fertility. The presence of more accessible land led to increased crop production, which eventually resulted in farmers developing methods of harvesting, storing, and protecting crops.

With an improved storage process, food became readily available, which led to a rise in the population in Yorubaland. The gradual increase in the population led to the emergence of settlements in more areas of the country. As the settlements increased, the forests separating the settlements from each other soon became open farmland.

The improvement and availability of tools gave rise to various professions and facilitated the division of labor. While farming was the main occupation of the Iron Age, some men became more involved in hunting due to greatly improved tools. From the onset, hunters were held in high regard. Apart from supplying the community with meat, other professions depended on them. For instance, potters and iron smelters depended on hunters to find good clay deposits. Also, the people relied on them to provide security against raiders and thieves and to help find clean brooks and streams. If there was a need for a group to relocate, the responsibility to find a new spot to settle and the best route to reach it usually fell on the hunters.

Another notable profession made possible by the Iron Age was the arts. Some of the earliest sculptures were done in terracotta. Also, the earliest wood carvings were made possible through the use of iron tools. Most of these carvings were used in house decorations as well as shrines.

As you can probably guess, the Iron Age had an impact on the economy. Iron tools improved the harvesting of oil palm trees, which was one of their major crops. The development of tools and skills helped the Yoruba farmers incorporate more crops into their farming. Among the many crops they planted was cotton, which opened up the weaving industry. The Yoruba also cultivated plants to use in dyeing cloths.

The coming of the Iron Age was a huge blessing, as it led to improved skills and better management of the environment. People learned how to build better and stronger homes, and this led to people erecting buildings that housed their extended families under the same roof. This birthed the concept of agbo-ile, a compound for the family that consisted of many homes with a number of courtyards around which the homes were positioned.

Architectural and aesthetic improvements to the agbo-ile turned it into a strong and safe haven. Plaster was used for the walls, which increased the safety and durability of the home. Also, weaving thatched roofs became an art, and the roofs would last for generations, with only the need for minor repairs. The agbo-ile gradually became a competition, with people trying to outdo each other in regard to decorations. These decorations also included shrines.

The rivalries between compounds resulted in artistic expressions like oriki. This is poetry in which each lineage glorifies itself and preserves its history. Facial markings also became a way to identify with one's ancestry. All of this contributed to the development of the Yoruba people's identity and distinctiveness, especially when it came to lineages and settlements.

The growth and development of the Yoruba society started with the smallest unit: the family. The oldest living male member of the family was seen as the leader. He was the keeper of the family's customs, secrets, and totems (objects treasured and passed down by the leaders of the family/group). The leader was seen as the family's spiritual guide and the one who tended to the family shrine. What started as a closely knit family soon grew into a large group bound by shared beliefs, values, and rules. At some point, the leader of each settlement began wearing objects that helped indicate they were the leader.

There were different types of organizations in the earliest settlements. Still, the most common was the age grade, which was used to provide appropriate tasks for the people in the agbo-ile, like keeping an open space clean. Over time, the concept of the age grade evolved and began to include new rules and regulations. Apart from one's compound or lineage, the age grade was one of the most popular ways to identify oneself among the early Yoruba people.

Most adult men were farmers and were assisted by their wives and children. A typical day in the agbo-ile started at dawn, where most men went out to their farm. Those who were left behind included the elderly, children, and those with a home-based occupation. The homebound people carried out domestic activities while the children played under the watchful eyes of the aged and nursing mothers. By the late afternoon, the farmers would return home, bearing produce and firewood. Dinner would be served in the evening, and the hours after dinner were used for socializing. The men conversed while sharing a keg of palm wine while the women performed light domestic chores. The children listened and told stories, usually folklore.

The agbo-ile was one of the building blocks of the economy. Each agbo-ile took produce to the village market, and some agbo-iles became known for the things they sold. One of the earliest modes of trade was bartering, although the Yoruba later used cowry shells as a form of payment.

One of the triumphs of the early Yoruba people was the development of traditional medicine. Over the centuries, each settlement accumulated knowledge of various herbs to treat illnesses. They also gained vast knowledge on the nature of different diseases. Each settlement had a professional herbalist that the people depended on for treatment. Over time, professional herbalists evolved into specialists, i.e., those specializing in treating mental diseases, delivery of babies, etc. Over the years, the settlements set up rules and regulations in regard to herbalists.

The birth of a baby was celebrated in the agbo-ile. For several weeks, the older women within the compound served as the baby's mother in what is called collective nurturing. They also helped the new mother by passing on their knowledge to her.

Children, both living and those yet unborn, were regarded as important members of the compound. It is believed that everything a lineage owned belonged to the next generation. This shows that the early Yorubas valued their children and invested heavily in their training and education. The next generation's education was a collective effort, and each agbo-ile raised their young in its image, with the people passing down their knowledge of their ancestral history. They also trained their young in their lineage's profession. For instance, some agbo-ile were known for a particular trade, and the people of the compound would often continue practicing it in the next generation.

Births were not the only celebrations in the agbo-ile. There were also village and lineage festivals, weddings, and funerals. The Yorubas celebrated weddings in a grand style. They involved three major activities:

the introduction ceremony, the betrothal ceremony, and the ceremonial journey of the bride back to her husband's agbo-ile. Nowadays, the Yoruba people call their wedding celebrations *owambe* and have simplified the ceremonies into just two: the introduction and the engagement.

The Yorubas believed in exogamy, which means marriages often occurred outside of one's family and clan. The Yorubas also practiced a patrilineal kinship system, whereby every child belonged to their father's lineage and could only inherit from that lineage. A woman married into a family from another compound automatically became her husband's family and could never revert to her father's family, even after her death.

Mourning was another event done collectively in the agbo-ile. Mourning could go on for days, especially if it was the death of a young adult. In the early days, most children died in infancy, and few made it to adulthood. The people always buried their dead in their compound.

Overall, the agbo-ile was one of the most important factors in the development of the early Yoruba civilization. Each agbo-ile had a system of government under the leadership of the olori-ebi, who acted as the ruler and the priest. Each village or settlement had a government with an exalted ruler, chiefs, rules, and laws guiding them.

Disputes and quarrels were settled by the olori-ebi (the oldest man in the village or compound), but he had the help of the elders. They exercised judicial and penal authority in all matters concerning the lineage. One of the olori-ebi's duties was to make room for members of the lineage to express their opinions.

The earliest Yorubas had a distinct religion, and they followed the religious guidance of the oldest member of the family. Also, as more occupations were established, patron gods and goddesses began to appear. Farmers, hunters, and market women all had a god or goddess attached to their profession. Deities were accepted and worshiped in Yorubaland.

The number of deities worshiped varied according to each settlement.

The Yoruba believed that all existence could be found in two realms: the lower realm and the upper realm. The upper realm consists of two spheres: a higher and a lower. The higher is overseen by Olodumare, the creator of all things. The second sphere, the one closer to humans, is the home to gods like Ifa, Ogun, and Obatala. Divination, the ability to tell the future, was an important part of the Yoruba culture. It was made possible through Ifa.

Another development in the Yoruba culture was the belief in the afterlife. The Yorubas believed that people who died went on to live in another realm. This explains why their dead were buried with articles of clothing. The root of their belief in the afterlife began with their idea that each individual has a minimum of three spiritual beings living within them. The first spirit, *emi*, resides in the heart and lungs and is powered by the winds entering the nostrils, the same way fire is powered by the wind produced by a blacksmith's bellows. The word *emi* can be translated as either "life" or "breath" because, without life, there is no breath. And without breath, there is no life. It is with *emi* that a man moves, walks, eats, speaks, sees, hears, and makes love.

The second spiritual being is *ojiji*, which means "shadow." Every individual is followed by their shadow throughout their life, and when he or she dies, the shadow also follows them to their final destination in the afterlife. The third being is called *eleda*, meaning "spirit." The *eleda* is regarded as the guardian soul of an individual, and it requires regular sacrifices to continue serving the individual.

These are the basic spiritual beings that all individuals must have to live. The other types of spiritual beings can be acquired at birth or over the course of one's lifetime by making agreements with the gods in charge of those beings. At death, these spiritual beings evacuate the body of the individual and await his or her presence in the afterlife. Apart from the beings, the individual is also welcomed by their family members who had already died.

A person's afterlife depended on the deeds they had done during their life. After dying, the *eleda* reports the person's earthly deeds to Olorun (the ruler of the heavens). The good souls are sent to Orun Rere ("Good Heaven"), and the wicked souls who are guilty of witchcraft, theft, or murder are sent to Orun Buburu ("Wicked Heaven") or Orun Apadi ("Hell Fire") as punishment.

Even though the missionaries introduced science and the Christian belief of the afterlife, there are still Yorubas who believe in the concept of having a guardian soul, *eleda,* that is in charge of their destiny; a shadow, *ojiji,* that follows them through life recording their actions; and an *emi* that gives them breath to live. There are about one hundred million practitioners of the Yoruba faith today.

Another popular belief in Yorubaland was (and still is) reincarnation. They believed that the dead would be reincarnated into one of their descendants, which is a belief that has influenced many Yoruba names. For instance, the name Babatunde is given to a male child whose grandfather died close to his birth, while Yetunde or Iyabo is given to a female child whose grandmother had passed away recently. The name Babatunde means "father has returned," and Yetunde or Iyabo translates to "mother has returned."

There is also the concept of akudaaya, which roughly translates to "death without leaving earth." This is similar to the concept of ghosts in other cultures. The difference is that the ghosts in Yorubaland go on to live new lives. They start new families and may possibly live until they die of old age. Not everyone who dies becomes an akudaaya, but if a person dies a wrongful death or before their predestined time of death, the chance of becoming one increases. After death, the person's soul leaves their body, travels to another village or town, and goes on living until their predestined time of death. The people in the new town are able to see and touch the individual, which means they view the akudaaya as just another person. However, the moment a single person becomes aware, the akudaaya flees and moves to another place to start all over. This is another belief that is still prevalent in present-day Yorubaland.

Chapter 3 – Deified Yoruba Heroes

The ancient Yoruba heroes were not just heroes; they were also kings turned gods, goddesses, and deities. The origin story of the Yorubas cannot be told without speaking of them. They were so revered that each of them had a dedicated group of people, agbo-ile, and villages that worshiped them. Before Britain colonized Nigeria, which brought about a massive missionary campaign, the primary religion of the Yorubas was idol worship. Some of their gods were Oduduwa, Shango, Ogun, Oya, and Oshun, although there were many, many more. These heroes are still worshiped today, but idol worship is now the minority among the Yorubas, with many people identifying as Christians or Muslims.

Oduduwa (Odùduwà)

It is only befitting that the first god to be discussed is Oduduwa, as he is one of the heroes who cannot be left out when discussing the Yorubas. Oduduwa was coined from the name *Odu ti o da Iwa*, meaning the "author of existence." Yoruba historians have stated that Oduduwa was the son of Olodumare. You might recall that Oduduwa was sent to earth via a chain; this earned him the name Atenworo, meaning "one who descends from a chain."

In the early days, Ile-Ife had close to thirteen communities, and each community had its own Oba (ruler or king). Oduduwa was popular among most of these communities, and this allowed him to overthrow Obatala, his brother, from the throne and take over. It also led to hostilities between Oduduwa and Obatala, the latter of whom had (according to some versions of the legend) founded Ile-Ife on orders from Olodumare, the supreme god.

Oduduwa changed the decentralized system of Ile-Ife to a centralized one and created the title of Ooni of Ife. Previously, there were thirteen Obas, but with Oduduwa's new title, there was only one ruler of Ife: Oduduwa.

Oduduwa lived a fulfilling life with a large family. He had multiple wives: Omonide (his favorite) and Adetinrin Anasin. He also had many children, including Orunto, Iyunade, Ajagunla, and Ifagbamila, just to name a few.

After Oduduwa's peaceful death, the Yorubas started to worship him. Human sacrifices were offered to him until the time of the British protectorate.

Ogun (Ògún)

Ogun was the Ooni of Ife after Oduduwa. He was skilled in metalwork, which earned him the title god of iron after his death. Ogun's expertise in hunting made people call him Osin-Imole, which means "chief among the divinities."

According to Ife mythology, when the other gods came to earth, Ogun cleared the path for them with a metal ax and had a dog as his companion. Ogun loved being alone on the hilltop, but when he was tired of his lonely life, he came down the hill, clothed in fire and blood. He wanted to mingle with the people, so he took fronds from a palm tree and went to Ire, where he was crowned king.

Ogun's death is interesting. His subjects refused to pay him the respect he wanted, so he killed them and then killed himself. But he wasn't buried. He disappeared into the earth, but he told his people that whenever they called him, he would answer.

Some parts of Yorubaland still offer sacrifices to Ogun. The main items used for sacrifice are iron and dogs because of his love for hunting and dogs.

Oranyan (Ọranyan)

Oranyan, also called Oranmiyan, was the grandson of Oduduwa and the son of Ogun. A peculiar fact about him is that he was birthed after his mother had an affair with both Ogun and Oduduwa; thus, he is known as the "man of two fathers."

His skin tone carved out his name. He was mostly light-skinned like his father, Ogun, but he was dark-skinned in some parts like his grandfather, Oduduwa. This led to the creation of the name Oranmiyan (*Oran ni omo ni yan*), meaning, "the child has chosen to be controversial."

Oranyan was brave and a great hunter. At that time, Ile-Ife had no military, so he took it upon himself to defend it. This made him the first Akogun (general) of Ife.

During one of the earliest wars, Obalufon Ogbogbodirin, the fourth Ooni of Ife, sent Oranyan off with his brother to conquer Igodomigodo (the historical name of the Benin Empire). Obalufon's aim was for Oranyan to die since Oranyan was giving him trouble.

Unfortunately for Obalufon, Oranyan didn't die; he actually won the war. But he didn't go back to Ife; instead, he stayed at Igodomigodo. However, he noticed that the people of Igodomigodo didn't like him. This made him uncomfortable, and he felt it was wrong to rule them when he wasn't from their land, so he left.

Before he left, he took the daughter of Egor's chief as his wife, and they had a child together named Eweka. Egor was located nearby, and the people accepted Eweka more willingly. He became the first Oba of Benin. (Some sources that Oranyan was the first ruler of Benin, who then passed the throne to his son so he could continue his explorations.)

Oranyan moved northward with his large army. Eventually, he found a secure place where he established the Oyo Empire, calling it Oyo-Ile. After conquering a nearby village, he took another wife.

Oranyan was a great traveler and explored many different places. After his adventures, he went back to Ile-Ife and demanded that the throne be handed to him, despite being Ogun's youngest son. Because Oranyan was a warrior and highly feared, the fifth Ooni of Ife stepped down so he could take over. He ruled for a short while, but eventually, he wanted to continue his adventure. So, he left the village. But before leaving, he told the people of Ile-Ife that if they needed him to protect them, they should make some incantations to summon him. He assured them that he would come to save them.

There was peace in Ile-Ife until Oranyan's enemies attacked the city. The people called out to Oranyan with the proper incantations, and he came back to fight for them. But while killing his enemies, he mistakenly killed some of his people, including his best friend. This left him devastated. Agonized by what he had done, he drove his staff into the ground and left on his horse. The Yorubas never saw him again.

Oranyan was a great warrior who successfully ruled two (possibly three) Yoruba kingdoms and established the Oyo Empire. The staff he left behind is now known as the Staff of Oranyan, and it is a tourist attraction that brings people from all over the world to Ile-Ife.

Ajaka

Ajaka, the son of Oranyan, was the only legendary king to reign the Oyo Empire twice, as he was removed from office and then called back to reclaim the throne. Even though warfare was the order of the day, Ajaka was a man of peace. Due to his calm nature, he was made to step down to allow his fierce brother, Shango, to rule.

After Shango's death, Ajaka was called back to reclaim the throne, but his rule must have surprised the people. He had changed a lot during the years, and he had become even fiercer than Shango. He killed the maternal relations of Shango with arrows mounted on birds. He waged war with literally everybody, including over one thousand of his chiefs and princes.

Ajaka had special people called medicine men who made charms for him. After the war, the medicine men requested to return to their homes, but Ajaka refused. He was afraid that other kings would request their services and that they would get charms as well. Seeing that Ajaka was not ready to let them go, the medicine men all vanished except for one, Elenre. Ajaka was furious, and he took his anger out on Elenre.

Ajaka attempted to kill Elenre, but all his attempts were futile until Ijaehin, Elenre's wife, told Ajaka what to do. Ijaehin told him to pull some grass from Elenre's roof to make him powerless. Another version of the story claims that it was Omoloja, one of Ajaka's maids who was sleeping with Elenre, who told Ajaka to decapitate Elenre with a sharp palm leaf blade.

Ajaka's men followed the directives provided by the snitch and then cut off Elenre's head. His head fell into Ajaka's hands, who caught it unconsciously. The head became stuck to his hand, and all attempts to take it off were worthless. This drained Ajaka because the head ate every food and drank brought to him. Ajaka was dying, and many magicians were called to neutralize the charm. Only one was able to succeed: Asawo.

When Asawo entered Ajaka's chambers, he prostrated himself before Elenre's head and explained that he had no other choice but to come because it was the king's request. By doing this, Asawo emphasized how powerful Elenre was, and he praised him for all his magic works and how he had defeated a lot of people.

Elenre was pleased with this and rolled off Ajaka's hand to form a river at Oyo called Odo Elenre ("Elenre's river"). His wife, Ijaehin, also formed a river at Oyo, but Elenre ordered the river to remain stagnant. The head incident caused Ajaka to make a rule that no king would be present at an execution in the future. There is no record of what happened to Ajaka after this event.

Shango (Ṣàngó)

Shango is the most popular orisha, which is a spirit known to interact with humans. Shango, also called Jakuta, was the second son of Oranyan. He was wild and had a fiery temper.

Shango's brother Ajaka was the ruler of the Oyo Empire before Shango came to power. The Olowu (the ruler) of the Owu Kingdom and Ajaka's cousin constantly intimidated Ajaka, making him appear less powerful to the people. The Olowu once forced Ajaka to pay tribute to him, despite the fact that Ajaka was also a king. This led to Ajaka's removal from the throne. Shango then took over, and when the Olowu asked Shango to pay tribute to him, Shango refused. This caused a fight, during which Shango made the Olowu and his army fear him by emitting smoke and fire from his mouth. They never bothered him again.

One day, Shango desired to worship at his mother's burial ground, but he was unable to because he didn't remember her name. His mother, the daughter of Elempe, a Nupe king, died when he was an infant. To obtain her name, Shango commissioned a Tetu (king executioner) and a Hausa slave. (There are varying accounts on the number and type of people he sent to Nupe.) They were to travel to the land of the Nupe, specifically where his mother was from, to offer the sacrifice of a cow and a horse for his mother. Their mission was to listen for his mother's name when the sacrifice was being offered.

Upon reaching the town, King Elempe entertained the men sent by his grandson and offered them drinks and food. The Hausa slave got drunk, but the Tetu was very careful and avoided drinking. When the sacrifice started, only the Tetu paid attention and heard Shango's mother's name when it was mentioned.

When the men returned to Oyo, the Tetu was rewarded with money since he knew the name of Shango's mother. The Hausa slave was punished. He was given 122 razor cuts for failing to follow Shango's instructions. When the cuts had healed, the women in the palace, including Shango's wives, thought they were beautiful. They told this to Shango, leading him to make a rule that every royal should bear these cuts. Being one of the royals, Shango handed himself over to the markers to cut him with the razor, but he could only bear two cuts on his arm. However, this gave him an idea.

Oko was a very powerful region, as it bore the central seat of the government. Shango wanted to bring this seat to Oyo, but he knew that the prince at Oko would refuse. So, he devised a strategy to use the Hausa slave's cuts to achieve his goal.

He sent the Hausa slave and the markers to the prince at Oko. They had to convince the royals of the beauty of these cuts. The royals saw the slave and believed that the marks would look good on them as well. The markers made the cuts on them while they performed some rites. On the third day, Shango attacked Oko and overtook it because the royals were too weak to fight. He transferred the seat of government from Oko to Oyo, just as he wanted.

Shango reigned for seven years, during which he made conquests and showed his strength. He also made charms. There was a particular one that he made that caused lightning. One day, he wanted to try a new experiment. He ascended Ajaka hill with his slaves and cousins, intending to try out this new idea of creating a storm with the charm. Although he thought the idea to be useless, it actually worked—a little too well, in fact. The charm started a storm, and lightning struck the palace, igniting a fire. Before they could descend the hill to quench the fire, many of Shango's wives and children had already died.

Seeing that Shango was the reason behind the whole misfortune, he was made to renounce his throne. He was then brought to the court of his grandfather, Elempe, King of the Nupes. Not all of his people were against him, though; some wanted a peaceful resolution to the matter, and they offered to help him find wives who could bear him children. But because Shango couldn't stand having even a single person being against him, he left Oyo with some followers, including his head slave and favorite servant, Biri.

However, Biri didn't like Shango's decision and encouraged Shango to turn back and start a new life with the wives that had been offered to him. Shango refused, and Biri left him. The other followers followed in Biri's footsteps. Shango was left alone, which devasted him further, resulting in him hanging himself on a shea tree.

His friends heard of his death, and they paid homage by burning his body and burying the remains under the same tree before also committing suicide one by one. Biri was the first to commit suicide, and he was followed by other slaves and some of Shango's cousins. The deaths ended with Shango's favorite wife, Oya.

Some say Shango didn't commit suicide but entered into the ground and disappeared. Another claim is that he transformed into an orisha by ascending to heaven on a chain. Shango is still worshiped in some parts of Yorubaland as the god of lightning and thunder.

Oshun (Ọṣun)

Oshun (also spelled as Osun) is another orisha. She is a river deity that represents femininity, fertility, and love. She was one of King Shango's wives. According to legend, she was sent to help Shango as an Irunmole, a spirit. It is said that the other Irunmoles sent to help the founding heroes create the world ignored Oshun and only started to respect her after Shango stood up for her.

There are two accounts of this story. One version claims that the female spirits sent to create the world wanted to be in control, but all their attempts were in vain because they lacked male approval. Another account asserts that the male Irunmoles wanted to create a world free from female influence. However, doing this caused the world to fail. The first version is probably a patriarchal interpretation of the second story, which is more in line with the reverence of feminine power by traditional orisha worshipers. Even though the versions contradict each other, they both end the same way, with Shango telling the spirits to respect Oshun the way they respected him.

She is celebrated at the Osun-Osogbo festival, which is named after a sacred grove near the Osun River. It is held annually every August for two weeks. The festival started seven hundred years ago after Oshun revealed herself to a hunter named Olutimehin and his followers when they settled at the bank of the Osun River to survive the famine that had driven them from their former settlement. Oshun instructed the people to move up the river to higher ground and promised them prosperity if they offered her an annual sacrifice. The place the people moved to is now known as the city of Osogbo, and the sacrifice is still offered to her annually. However, the Osun-Osogbo festival is now more than just offering sacrifices. It is recognized as an international event, as it attracts worshipers and tourists from all over the world. The festival receives visitors from countries such as Brazil, Trinidad, Cuba, Jamaica, Tobago, Spain, the United States, and

Canada.

Oya

Oya was the youngest wife of Shango. Her powers were rooted in the natural world, and she controlled lightning, thunder, rainstorms, tornadoes, and hurricanes. What made her stand out amongst the other goddesses was her ability to relate with other women. Although she was a loving and caring mother, she could also transform into a fierce warrior in an instant.

Oya is venerated around the world. Some know her to be the guardian of the realms of life and death. Hence, she controlled activities related to death like funerals and spiritual communication, as well as reincarnation and psychic abilities. Her ability to call out or drive away the spirit of death made people fear her. Since Oya was the goddess of the wind, she gives the first breath humans take, but she also takes their last breath.

As the goddess of rain, Oya gave her husband the power to create storms, so storms followed whenever she and her husband walked together. This could be anything from gentle to violent rainstorms capable of bringing down strong buildings.

Oya met her husband in a forest. He came to kill a buffalo that he had been stalking for some time. Before he could strike a blow, the buffalo suddenly turned into a woman. He took her home, named her Oya, and then married her. Oya and Shango loved each other to the point that Oya followed Shango on his conquests. And when Shango died, Oya was so sad that she hid among a sheep flock to avoid being found before gathering the courage to join her husband in death (or disappearance, as some accounts say). This action makes her worshipers avoid eating sheep meat.

Oya sometimes changed to a buffalo, and when she left the earth, she pulled one of her horns out and gave it to her children. Every year, people offer buffalo horns to the shrines of Oya so that she may continue guiding them and bless them with favors. These people are called the "Children of Buffalo."

Aganju

Aganju is another orisha, and he is associated with the sun and volcanoes. It is not known if the real Aganju has any connection to the mythical one. Some historians believe it might just be a coincidence that the two shared the same name.

Regardless, Aganju, the ruler of Oyo, was brave, and during his reign, he built houses and improved the lives of the people. His reign was prosperous until he fell in love with the daughter of another king. He waged war with this king for not allowing him to marry his daughter. The war claimed many lives, and during the war, Aganju killed his heir, Lugbe, because he caught him having an affair with Iyayun, his wife. Aganju suffered for years due to what he had felt forced to do, and he eventually died of grief.

Aganju's exact relationship with Shango is unclear, but there appears to be some sort of relationship between them. Some say that Aganju was the father of Shango, while others say that they were brothers.

Chapter 4 – The Kingdoms of Yorubaland

There were many founding kingdoms in Yorubaland; however, not all are going to be mentioned in this chapter, as those other kingdoms are discussed extensively in other chapters. The Yoruba kingdoms are best divided into three geographical regions to better understand how each kingdom was established and flourished. These divisions are the central, southern, and eastern kingdoms.

Map of major Yoruba cities
CommonRollebon (talk) and Commons, CC BY-SA 3.0 <http://creativecommons.org/licenses/by-sa/3.0/>, via Wikimedia Commons https://commons.wikimedia.org/wiki/File:HistoYoruba.jpeg

The Central Kingdoms

Territories in the central kingdoms include the Ife, Ilesha, Ifewara, and Owu kingdoms.

The Ifewara Kingdom

Ifewara was founded almost a century after the establishment of Ile-Ife. It was situated toward the southeast of the prominent Ife Kingdom by Prince Olojo Agbele. Olojo Agbele had failed to secure the throne of Ile-Ife, so he left with his followers to a settlement not too far from Ife. The people in the settlement received him warmly and joined his followers to crown him as king. The new king called the new town Ifewara, meaning "Ife that is full of milk and honey."

Most of the beliefs and traditions that were practiced in Ile-Ife were replicated in Ifewara. For instance, both kingdoms had chiefs bearing the same titles, such as Obalufe and Obajio, and the same functions and respect were accorded to these chiefs precisely as it was done in Ife. Also, deities and celebrations were performed in the same manner. Ifewara was basically a smaller replica of Ile-Ife.

The people of Ifewara sought to be more recognized and come out of the shadow of their more prominent neighbor, so they demanded to have their kings wear a beaded crown. This was rejected by the Ooni of Ife in 1916. Ifewara strengthened its relationship with Ilesha; soon enough, they became independent of Ife. They asked the Owa of Ilesha to grant them permission to use a beaded crown. The Owa granted the request in 1946; however, the citizens of Ifewara protested against their ruler, claiming they were not under Ilesha rule either. By asking for permission, the people saw their king acting as subservient to the Owa.

The Ilesha Kingdom (Ijesha Kingdom)

Most Yoruba kingdoms believe they originated from Ife. The Ijeshas (who populated the Ilesha Kingdom) are not exempted from this group.

The Ijeshas had many cities, such as Ilesha, Otan, Ipetu Jesa, Esa-Oke, and Imesi-Ile, which are generally found toward Ife's east. Ilesha was more prominent than the others.

Like most Yoruba kingdoms, an Ife prince by the name of Ajibogun established Ijeshaland after his journey to the coast to get some seawater, which had been recommended for Oduduwa's eye defects. According to tradition, Oduduwa was Ajibogun's grandfather. This quest was not easy, and Oduduwa feared that his grandson might never return, so he gave his remaining male heirs gifts and tokens to start their own kingdoms away from Ife. However, Ajibogun was still alive, and upon his return from the coast with the seawater, Oduduwa, grateful for his grandson's successful quest, gave him his sword known as Ida Ajase, meaning "sword of victory," as a token. Ajibogun took the sword and headed east toward the Ijesha forest with his followers. They settled in Igbadaiye; some scholars believe Ajibogun died there.

There are other versions of Ajibogun's story. Others say he became involved in conquests. He stayed in Ilemure, which he gave to his son Ooyela. This town was eventually named Ilu Obokun (Obukon is another name that is used in place of Ajibogun in the stories), and today, it is known as Ibokun.

The spirit of conquest continued for some time. The kings ruled Oke-Osun, Iwori, Ipole, and Ejioro before finally settling in Ilesha, with their king now called an Owa. During their journey to Ilesha, the conquerors encountered other settlements like Akogun, Ibosirin, Igbogi, Lurere, Asore, and Okesa, which collectively agreed to acknowledge the Owa as their king.

The Owa met a farmer in Okesa who grew okra (ila), a staple food for the king and his entourage. The title of Obanla (king of Okra-ila) was given to the farmer. Obanla became one of the highest titles in Ilesha, and he was the second in command to the Owa.

Another important position in the Ilesha Kingdom was the Ogboni of Obokun. The title was given to the ruler of Obokun before the Owa left for Ilesha. The Obokun had a shrine that had to be visited before a new Owa could be installed. There, rituals would be performed, likely blessing the king with a prosperous reign. This was done to pay homage to the fact that the people of Ilesha can trace themselves to Obokun.

The Eastern Kingdoms

The Yoruba kingdoms moved eastward, beyond the hills and forests of Ilesha. These are the Ekiti and Akoko kingdoms. The Ekiti people have many small kingdoms identified in their history, like Ado, Ikole, Ijero, Ikere, Otun, Efon, Ogotun, Ire, and Obo. The prominent ones of historical significance are discussed in this chapter.

The Ire Kingdom

This kingdom gained prominence in Yoruba history as the original home of Ogun, the god of iron. The first ruler of Ire, the Onire, was a high priest of Ogun, and the people believed that they evolved from him. Some Yoruba traditions confirm the Ire people originated from Ogun.

Ire was believed to be very powerful, so when some of the kingdoms were subduing other settlements and merging towns, they left Ire alone. This brought peace, stability, and prosperity to the kingdom at a time when migration and conquests were a common occurrence.

The Ado Kingdom

Immigrant princes who were either denied the throne or left their home kingdom to establish their own communities founded most of the Yoruba kingdoms. Ado was one of the kingdoms established this way.

The founder was an Ife prince known as Awamaro, meaning the "restless one," and he had the title of Ewi, meaning the "speaker." Awamaro left Ife with his brother Oranyan (yes, the famous ruler mentioned above) to Benin. After some years of living there, Awamaro left Oranyan in Benin and journeyed north with his followers. Due to his restlessness, he also journeyed east as far as the Ekiti forests. He was urged to stop at Agbado by the older people in his group. They knew they could not continue on with Awamaro, so this group chose to settle in Agbado.

Relentless in his journey, Awamaro continued east until he arrived at a settlement surrounding the spiritual Olota Rock. The power of the rock was thought to be controlled by the Elesun of Ilesun; the Elesun was the chief priest and also the protector of the area by the Olota Rock.

After arriving in Ilesun, Awamaro and his followers settled and lived with the people there peacefully until clashes erupted between them. During the fighting, Awamaro subdued his opponent, the Elesun, and cut off his head before establishing the Ado Kingdom and taking the title Ewi of Ado. The Elesun's influence in Ado is still seen today, with each succeeding Ewi paying obeisance at the Elesun's grave before assuming the throne.

The leaders in Awamaro's group and those of the older settlement became the chiefs of the Ado Kingdom. Centuries later, the people of Ila also joined the Ado Kingdom. The leader of Ila, known as the Alarierin, was later made a chief in the Ado Kingdom. The people of Ila were originally from the Ila Orangun Kingdom formed by one of the male descendants of Oduduwa. It was part of the first seven kingdoms established by the Oduduwa bloodline that departed from Ife.

The Ikere Kingdom

The Ikere Kingdom was known to have challenges with its leadership. By the late 17th century, the challenges brought an internal change in the leadership structure of the Ikere Kingdom. Like other established kingdoms, the creator of Ikere migrated from Ife but was later dethroned by a trusted friend, Ogoga, who was a famous Edo hunter living in Ikere.

The Olukere, besides being the king of Ikere, was also the priest of the Olosunta Rock; Olosunta was regarded as the highest deity in the land. The Olukere was in charge of the rituals at the shrine, and due to his busy schedule, he was said to have instructed Ogoga to help attend to administrative issues like judging disputes between the townspeople. This led to the usurpation of the Olukere's power and authority, although how Ogoga did this is not clearly understood. Ogoga became the king while the ousted Olukere became the high priest of the kingdom.

The Akure Kingdom

The princes from Ife always moved out of the kingdom to establish a new settlement. This was the case with Akure, which was established by Omoremilekun Asodeboyede, an Ife prince. Asodeboyede wandered around the forests of Efon and Ara before settling in Akure.

Akure was founded along the route going from Ife to modern-day Edo State. Asodeboyede conquered all of the nearby settlements, such as Oke-Aro, Idopetu, Obanla, Ijomu, and Ilemo. He combined these settlements and established his new kingdom in the most fertile and productive part of the forest.

Akure received its name from a historical event that occurred during that period. When Asodeboyede got to this location, the array of royal beads around his neck suddenly came loose. This led to his follower exclaiming, "Akun re!" meaning "The beads have snapped!" Thus, the settlement was named Akun re, and over time, it changed into Akure.

Deji is the official title of the Akure kings, but initially, they were called Ajapada. This title came about when Oba Olofinleyo married the daughter of the Oba of Ijeshaland. The princess gave birth to a son while her father was still on a pilgrimage. When he returned, he gifted the baby a small diadem. This act gave the child his praise name, which is found in oriki (praise poetry). The young boy was named Owafadeji, meaning "Owa gifted him a diadem." This name would stick with him until adulthood. By the time he became a king, the praise name had become the title of those who ruled Akure, as subsequent kings would later take Deji as their official title. However, even today, Ajapada remains a part of the Deji's ceremonial title.

The king's palace was built in 1150 CE in the center of the town. Akure was mostly independent throughout its history; however, at one point, they were subject to other kingdoms like the Kingdom of Benin and paid tribute to them. Benin used the Akure Kingdom as a base for trading, and subsequent Akure rebellions were put down. In the early 19th century, Akure briefly gained its independence from Benin rule, but it was conquered once more. The Deji was killed for his participation in the rebellion.

Akure and other Ekiti towns also became subject to Ibadan, a city located in southwestern Nigeria, in 1854. Akure endured Ibadan rule for about twenty years; in 1876, the Akure Kingdom rebelled and received its freedom during the following war between the principal Yoruba states.

Akoko Kingdoms

The Akoko countryside had hills similar to Ekiti, but they were more rugged. Unlike the Ekiti, whose settlers came from Ile-Ife, history revealed that the Akoko region had settlers who did not speak Yoruba. There was a different mix of people, with the Edo, Yoruba, Afenmai, and Nupe coming together to trade or try to establish settlements.

The Akoko area was provided natural defenses by the hilly countryside. The region frequently saw military campaigns from its neighbors like the Edo, Nupe, and Owo people, so the region could not boast of kingdoms as big and prosperous as the Ekiti countryside.

The kingdoms established in Akoko follow the same trend as most of the other Yoruba towns, with people migrating from another place. The princes of Benin who lost the throne or who enjoyed exploring often came to this region to conquer and establish new kingdoms. Many towns in Akoko, like Ishua, Ipe, Arigidi, Ifira, Ipesi, Afa, and Epeme, can connect their foundation to the Kingdom of Benin.

Most of these kingdoms, in the earlier stages of their history, did not operate a monarchy form of government like the Yoruba, but due to the constant displacement of people because of military campaigns, they adopted the Yoruba monarchy structure. During the prolonged war between the Yoruba principal states, Akoko, unlike the Ekiti people, did not experience most of the war since its rugged terrain acted as a natural defense against the Ibadan cavalry coming from the south. In addition, the bravery of the Akoko people helped to protect most of the towns.

The Southern Kingdoms

These kingdoms occupied territories closer to the Atlantic coast, and the regions were covered with thick forests. The kingdoms found here are Ilaje, Ikale, Ondo, Ijebu, Awori, Itsekiri, and Owo.

The Owo Kingdom

Owo was founded by an Ife prince named Asunlola Ojugbelu (also known as Omolaghaye). He was one of Orunmila's sons. (Orunmila was an orisha responsible for knowledge, divination, and wisdom.)

History revealed that Ojugbelu left Ife around the 12th century. Ojugbelu and his followers did not take the expected route but went through Idanre, where they stopped in places like Uji and Upafa. However, the group could not establish their kingdom in this location for several reasons, such as bad weather, extreme hostility from prior settlers, difficult terrain, and the lack of food and water. They tried again in another location called Ugbo Ogwata, but it also didn't work out. Eventually, though, they got to an old route that stretched from Ife to Benin. They decided to establish their kingdom, Owo, along this route. However, it was Imade, the son of Ojugbelu, who brought the group to this spot because Ojugbelu had died in Upafa.

Upon arriving at this location, they met settlements that were already established. These settlements include Okese, Omu, Oko, Efene, Ilale, Utelu, Igbe, and Idasen. The group led by Imade founded three early settlements, but they were often overcome. The Olomu of Omu chased Imade and his followers from the area. Efene, which was ruled by the Elefene, was the strongest of the three settlements, and it also repelled the newcomers. Idasen was one of the few settlements that received the migrants peacefully; however, adversity arose there when the migrants tried to assert authority over the other settlements, which led to hostilities.

Imade and his group were still able to establish their new kingdom amidst all the conflicts. The three aforementioned settlements attempted to unify other settlements against Imade. This prolonged fighting went on for many generations, and eventually, some settlements were overcome. Those who were friends with the new kingdom merged with it, with their leaders becoming chiefs. Owo grew and expanded slowly while later absorbing all the other settlements. They were forced to acknowledge the authority of the Olowu of Owo as their leader. Each settlement had its quarters controlled by their former leaders, who were now chiefs in the larger Owo Kingdom.

The Ode-Itsekiri Kingdom

This kingdom was established along some of the coastal lagoons, although there are reservations about how they got to this area and the origins of their monarchy. It is assumed that a Yoruba sub-group went as far as this region during the general expansion of the Yoruba people. However, their traditions are closely related to that of the Edo people.

Their origin can be traced to a Benin prince called Iginuwa. After he lost the throne to other competitors, he journeyed to the western delta. He met some Yoruba people who had already settled there. These earlier settlers accepted Iginuwa as their king, but the reason for this is actually not known. Many theories have sprung up over the years, with one being that Iginuwa impressed the established settlers with his royal regalia. It is also possible that the bilingualism of the Benin court played a major factor. Iginuwa might have spoken both Edo and Yoruba, making it easier for the Yoruba settlers to accept him.

The kingdom was quite diverse, absorbing the Edo, Ijaw, and Urhobo languages and cultural elements. Nevertheless, Yoruba remained its main language, which shows the dominance of the Yoruba people in the area before the arrival of Iginuwa. The capital of the new kingdom was called Ode-Itsekiri, which was similar to what the neighboring Yoruba kingdoms, like Ilaje and Ikale, called their towns.

The Ilaje Kingdom

The Ilaje group created their settlements along the coast, sharing borders with the coastal Ijebu people. They were also the closest Yoruba neighbors of the Itsekiri people. They occupied lagoons and creeks, which made the conglomeration of their population in a particular location largely impossible. However, they still had some kind of monarchy in place.

During the general Yoruba expansion, the Ilaje people created two kingdoms: a western kingdom with its capital in Mahin and an eastern kingdom with its capital in Ugbo. It is thought that the Ugbo Kingdom was the older of the two.

The economy of the Ilaje people was based on fishing and trading since they lived, for the most part, around water. The worship of water deities and other Yoruba gods was deeply rooted in their culture. According to tradition, these spirits were usually involved in disputes over fishing rights, trade, accusations of stealing, and many other things. The most prominent among these spiritual deities was Ayelala, and the most popular shrine of hers was found along the Oluwa River. She is still widely feared among the Ilaje communities today because of her severe punishments of dishonesty.

The Ikale Kingdom

The Ikales shared a boundary with the Ilajes along the coast, but southward, the land was mostly thick forests divided by water bodies. Most southern Ikale towns had once been camps in the forest that later became small kingdoms.

The Ikale Kingdom had a strong cultural influence from Benin, which could be seen in their chieftaincy titles and monarchy system. This influence was due to Benin's commercial expansion. The most prominent Ikale towns were Ode-Aye, Ode-Erinje, Osooro, Ode-Irele, and Ikoya, the latter of which is thought to be the first of the Ikale cities.

The Ikale generally engaged in trade by bartering with the Ilaje for fish and other products in exchange for agricultural staple foods like yam, cassava, and oil.

The Ondo Kingdom

The Ondo Kingdom was situated between Ikale and Ife. It was located in an area with thick forests and hills. Due to this, human settlement in this area was widely dispersed. And since the settlements were spaced away from each other, the people's dialect was markedly different in each settlement. Only three kingdoms were founded in this forest: Ondo, Idanre, and Epe.

We already know how Ondo was established, as its origin was discussed earlier in Chapter 1. The founders of Idanre were said to be Ife migrants who settled in the hilly area. Because they were mostly isolated from the other kingdoms, they did not fully imbibe the culture of the Ife migrants. Epe was originally a forest discovered by hunters from Ile-Ife. Epe is located close to Ijebu-Ode.

Chapter 5 – The Economy of the Early Yoruba Kingdoms

The early Yoruba kingdoms were thriving in terms of the economy. The people participated in various activities such as farming, trading, craft specialization, hunting, fishing, and owning domestic animals. The early Yoruba kingdoms ran a patrilineage system; skills and crafts were passed down through the father's family line. As a result, lineages became known for a particular skill and/or craft set.

The development of the Yoruba economy can be divided into two eras, with the first one being the precolonial era, which spanned from the 11th century to the early 16th century. This era took place before European involvement in Yorubaland. The second era would be kickstarted with the arrival of European traders at the beginning of the 16th century, and it would last until the 19th century.

The Precolonial Era (11th century to the early 16th century)

The creation of many cities, kingdoms, and towns in Yorubaland acted as a helpful catalyst in the transformation of its economic life in the 15th century. The Yoruba communities already had a form of a simple trade structure as early as the 11th century in the form of a barter system. As their civilization progressed, cowries were used as a form of payment. Soon, it became established as the main currency, and it was used for both commercial and social payments.

The Second Era (The early 16th century to the 19th century)

When the European coastal trade started in the early 16th century, it transformed many Yoruba kingdoms, ultimately shaping their economy. The transatlantic trade began with the slave trade. This aided the development of long-distance trade relations between the Europeans, Americans, and the early Yoruba people.

Later on, legitimate trade replaced the slave trade in the coastal regions. The kingdoms became a collection point for cocoa, palm oil, and kernels. These goods were brought to Lagos from inland kingdoms like Oyo and Benin, where it was then exported to Europe. During this period, trade with the Europeans was conducted only through Oyo, thus making it a monopolistic affair. Before any traders or merchants could conduct business with the Europeans, the Alaafin of Oyo had to issue a royal license.

The Kingdoms and Their Economic Framework

As mentioned earlier, many activities contributed to the development of the Yoruba kingdoms' economic framework. The emergence of the royal cities, kingdoms, and other major towns widened opportunities in other occupations, such as house building, arts, entertainment, priestly occupations, health care and herbal occupations, and, perhaps most importantly, commerce. All of these later aided the development of the

Yoruba civilization.

Agriculture

The early Yoruba people carried out many economic activities, but the most predominant one was farming. Communities engaged in the production of crops mostly for feeding the local populace, but they also did so for commercial purposes. These goods were exchanged or sold for cowries in local and distant markets for materials they could not produce.

Agriculture had always been a pillar of the economy, even before most Yoruba kingdoms were created. While agriculture was not the only activity they engaged in, it constituted a large portion of their economy. One reason agriculture thrived in Yorubaland was the combination of suitable soils and adequate rains. This made most of the Yoruba homeland ideal for this activity. However, not all of the Yoruba lands were suitable for this purpose; there were places with lagoons, creeks, and swamps that were just not suitable for some crop types. These areas were the homes of the Ilaje, Itsekiri, Ijaw, and Ikale people.

The other belt, close to the north—the home of the Ekiti, Owo, Ondo, Ijebu, and Egba kingdoms—produced crops like yams, cassava, and cocoa. Yams also grew well in Ekiti and Akoko. One of the reasons for this was that these towns were located in partly forest and partly grassland areas. These greatly influenced the type of crop produced. For instance, the grasslands were best for cereal crops (mostly millet, maize, and guinea corn) and some beans. Therefore, foods and delicacies made from cereals and beans featured more prominently in the diets of those living there.

Oil palm was another crop that was often grown by the Yoruba people; however, these trees thrived more in regions with lightly forested areas. Palm oil and palm wine are the two most important byproducts of this tree, and they were used daily by most Yoruba people. However, other materials like oil palm fronds could be gotten from oil palm trees. Fronds are the main material used in making roofs, mats, and other craftwork.

Another crop grown for agricultural purposes was the kola nut, known as *Obi Abata* in Yoruba. Kola nuts grew in all parts of Yorubaland, but the first kingdom to produce it in large quantities for exportation was the Ife Kingdom. Later on, the exportation of kola nuts would spread to other parts of Yorubaland, like Ilesha, Owu, Ijebu, and Egba. The farming and large-scale production of bitter kola, known in Yoruba as *orogbo*, also developed the same way. In areas like Ekiti, Oyo, and Ilesha, a particular bean tree grew, which yielded a bean called iru. This bean had a highly sought-after aromatic flavor. Indigo was also cultivated in commercial quantities and used to dye clothing.

The early Yoruba people also engaged in livestock farming. In some parts of Oyo, it was common for rich folks to own herds of cattle, goats, and sheep, which they reared and sold. This was done on a larger scale, so the owners required the help of laborers. The workers could have included both paid employees and slaves, and they could have come from within or beyond the kingdom. Most Yoruba people practiced the domestic rearing of livestock; however, this was done mainly by women. Some of the livestock included ducks, goats, sheep, pigeons, and chickens, most of which were reared in their homes, compounds, and/or neighborhoods. Some of the rich women had much livestock, which fetched them a considerable income.

Commerce and Trade

The Yoruba trade practices put them ahead of other kingdoms, especially over landlocked towns and settlements. As early as the 16th century, there was already an established trade relationship between the Yoruba kingdoms and the Europeans. The region was well diversified in terms of agricultural products, which led to a specialization in production and manufacturing. Also, the Yorubas were blessed with some mineral resources. These specializations boosted the volume of internal trade, leading to increased productivity in the agricultural and industrial sectors.

This increased productivity also led to a large number of products being exported beyond the Yoruba lands.

The Yoruba kingdoms became great places to trade, with their women ranking among the best traders in Africa. As productivity increased, long-distance trading surfaced, although the elites mostly carried it out during this period. Each Yoruba city had a king's marketplace, which was a way to generate, receive, distribute, and send out goods on a large scale. Cash crops and food crops like cocoa, kola nuts, and oil palms were all produced in mass quantities. This was aided by the region's topography, good weather, and high-quality soil.

The Yoruba trading empire covered many kingdoms and extended as far as the Senegal River in the west and the Congo to the east. Even within the Yoruba empire itself, many trading communities and routes were established. Two good examples are the Hausa and Nupe trading communities. Also, traders from the far north, like the Sahara, became a daily part of the trading communities. The Yoruba held the Nupe and Hausa traders in high regard, and they went out of their way to allocate space inside or close to the palace or marketplace for these traders.

As time went on, there was an increase in the number of Hausa and Nupe traders frequenting the Yoruba markets. Since many of the Hausa traders were Muslim, the kings gave them land to erect their own mosque, which was usually close to the marketplace. This made it easy for them to observe their prayer break, as they would be close to their stores or market stalls. Other communities in eastern and southern Yorubaland provided residences for these foreign traders. Through trade, the northerners were able to spread the Muslim religion to the Yorubas.

As you can see, many Yoruba kingdoms' economies and trade were something to behold back then. It certainly seems that they could hold their own among the best.

Manufacturing and Production

The exponential growth of the Yoruba economy gave rise to the manufacturing and production sector. This played a huge role in the development of many communities within Yorubaland.

The agricultural boom and subsequent storage problems led to many products being converted into something new. Crops like maize, cassava, and millet were used to manufacture new food delicacies. Maize was converted to pap, which could be in a semi-liquid form (*ogi*) or a solid form (*eko* or *agidi*). This delicacy was mostly manufactured in the Osun and Oyo region, from where it was exported to neighboring kingdoms and regions.

Processing cassava tubers into other products was also a productive and lucrative business for all the Yoruba kingdoms. The cassava tuber is still one of the most valuable plant products in West Africa. About 250,000 tons of garri (the creamy flour made from cassava) are prepared in Nigeria yearly. Cassava originated from South America, and it was made known to Nigerians in the 16th century by European colonizers from Portugal while trading for slaves. Its value was not truly known until freed slaves started returning in the early 19th century and introduced new processing methods for the crop. Cassava is a very versatile product that can be processed into different things, including fufu (a sticky dough), garri, animal feed, starches for gluing papers, and textiles.

Garri is the most common byproduct of cassava, and it is made by slicing and grating the tubers, then soaking and fermenting them for a few days before grinding and finally frying the cassava flakes. Garri has many health benefits because it contains phosphorus, calcium, and riboflavin. The starch in cassava is called resistant starch, which is good for industrial sizing and gluing purposes. The Yoruba kingdoms made a lot of income from cassava byproducts by exporting them to other regions. This had a positive impact on the Yoruba kingdoms' commerce at the time.

Another craft that boosted their commercial activities was cloth dyeing. This craft was usually passed from mother to daughter for many generations. Towns close to the Osun Valley were known for their beautiful and excellent dye work. Dyed clothes became an important fashion trend during the Second Era, with the demand for this product increasing across the regions as time passed. Some of the techniques employed in this production process include tie-dye. This involves tying the cloth into different shapes before dipping it into the dye. The demand for this product significantly boosted the trade of the Osun region.

In the early years of the Yoruba kingdoms, the production of jasper and carnelian beads came into the spotlight, especially in the Oyo and Ife kingdoms. These beads were worn mainly by royals, chiefs, and prominent figures in society. They were worn on the wrists, necks, and ankles, and they signified honor, power, authority, and prestige for the wearer. It was also believed that the beads would bring them good fortune. The production of these beads was a laborious process, and it required skill, strength, and considerable patience. Findings indicate that it could take professionals about four to seven days, with ten hours of dedicated work each day, for one bead worker to produce a necklace containing eighteen to twenty beads.

Beads represented one's power, so if someone increased their station, they would wear different beads to show this. Jasper was the preferred gemstone to signify power. Later on, some other gems, like carnelian and the red and brown chalcedonic quartzes, would come into play. Several varieties of these beads have been found in Oyo, Ile-Ife, Ilesha, and Benin. Due to the importance attached to these beads, they become desirable and valuable, making the production of beads a lucrative and attractive one, thus increasing the economic revenue of the kingdom at large.

Involvement of the Europeans and the Slave Trade

The trade relationship between the European and African nations developed in the economic era of the African continent. For West Africa, especially in the Gulf of Benin and along its coasts, the European merchants had a well-established trading population regulated by intelligent and experienced African rulers. Some goods imported to West Africa in large volumes included cloth, iron, raw copper, and cowry shells, the latter of which was used as a medium of exchange by the local populations along the West African coast. Other luxury items, such as jewelry, alcohol, and mirrors, were also imported.

The Portuguese were the first to arrive in West Africa when they were sailing around the Atlantic to seek a path into Africa that reached Asia. They arrived on the coast of Benin in the late 15th century. At that time, the Kingdom of Benin and most of the Yoruba kingdoms had already become quite advanced; for instance, kingdoms like Ife, Ondo, Oyo, and some Ekiti kingdoms were already trading on a large scale.

The Portuguese set up a factory (a trading post) at the Benin port town of Ughoton and in other places like Ode-Itsekiri. Later on, more trading posts were established by the Europeans along the Gulf of Benin. The Portuguese traders were also charmed by the island of Eko, which they would later rename Lagos. However, access to the island was very difficult due to the sand bars and dunes surrounding it.

This wasn't the only problem the Europeans faced. Even with the availability of factories in Yorubaland, none could serve as a natural harbor for large ships. And even if there was, the Ijebu and Ilaje coasts weren't as accessible as Lagos. Thus, the major European trade centers with the Yoruba interior kingdoms weren't located on the Yoruba coastline but rather in the Kingdom of Benin. Nevertheless, there were still some trading posts on the Yoruba coast, mainly on Lagos and the Ijebu coast; these grew gradually during the 16th century.

Later on, in the early 18th century, the European started a new port in Badagry, which is close to Lagos. However, when compared to Ughoton, it was relatively smaller. Still, it would still serve its purpose, as goods could easily reach the interior parts of the Yoruba kingdoms from Badagry.

When Badagry first started, it was mostly used for slave trading, which brought the Atlantic market closer to the Egba and Ijebu coasts in southern Yorubaland. The transatlantic slave trade commenced during the 15th century when Portugal and other European kingdoms first landed on the shores of West Africa. The Portuguese started kidnapping some of the natives of these regions, who were then taken back to Europe and sold into slavery.

Consequently, this resulted in the early development of Ijebu because it had access to the Europeans and their imports, which eventually opened up Osun and other frontiers to the Atlantic slave trade. The Ijebu traders were the top transporters of European imports, obtaining mostly cowries, tobacco, and textiles, in particular damask and silk materials.

The practice of slavery had long been established in Europe, as Europeans had enslaved each other for thousands of years. And this practice also already existed in Yorubaland long before the Europeans landed on the West African coast. However, the practice of buying and selling slaves was extremely rare. As of then, slaves, known as an *eru*, were only gotten as spoils of war. Often, the slaves would end up as palace servants or maids. Sometimes, the king might reward slaves to the worthiest of his cabinet and some of those who made the conquest possible. Thus, the Yoruba people owned slaves, but buying or selling them was not in vogue before the Europeans arrived.

Also, if an *eru* was allocated to the palace, he could have risen in rank depending solely on his character, loyalty, and strength. In Yorubaland, an *eru* may have become influential enough to the extent of marrying a princess. The men who didn't serve inside the palace may have been allowed to raise crops of their own on his master's farmland or establish some other enterprise; of course, he needed permission to do so. Unless he had some serious character blemish, he would usually inherit some of his master's belongings.

At the peak of the transatlantic slave trade, these *erus*, which were obtained through war, were sold as slaves. In the precolonial era, there were many Yoruba traders, but few eventually became wholesalers, who were referred to as an *alajapa*. These *alajapas* had rankings, and their leaders formed an association called the Parayoki, meaning "merchant's guild." Slave trading was an expensive endeavor, as it involved paying for the welfare and transportation of the slaves, traders, and soldiers. The soldiers were necessary to control the slaves and also to launch warfare on villages to capture more slaves.

War chiefs and politicians usually had soldiers working for them. Some of these soldiers were free and chose to work for their bosses; however, the majority of them were usually *erus* captured during previous wars. These soldiers were then sent to battle neighboring villages or communities that were known to be weak. After the battle, the war chief would lay claim to 40 to 60 percent of the slaves captured by the free soldiers and 60 to 80 percent of the slaves captured by the *eru* soldiers. The war chief could then sell these slaves with the help of traders and *alajapas*. The soldiers themselves also made money by selling the slaves to the Parayoki.

The traders would then transport these purchased slaves to the markets and ports to be purchased by the Europeans. The traders ensured their safe transport by employing soldiers. The Europeans, in turn, ensured the capture of slaves by providing weapons to the traders, who proceeded to sell those weapons to the soldiers. This way, all parties worked together to guarantee the flow of slaves. And on top of this, the Europeans and the traders also forged relationships and made alliances. Examples of some of the alliances include marriage arrangements, child fostering, and written contracts. These all continued until around the 1860s.

Institutions and Features That Aided the Yorubaland's Economy

While the Yoruba economy was a booming one, special institutions boosted it and made everything well organized.

Royal Finances

As with most monarchies, the royal finances were taken from tolls and taxes on commerce. All merchandise was taxed, except those obtained from peasants or local farmers. The king appointed an *onibode*, meaning "gatekeeper," to guard the kingdom and collect these taxes. His office was an important one, and it often became a hereditary position in most kingdoms.

The amount of revenue generated from tolls depended on the volume of trade passing through the kingdom's gates. The more accessible and safer a route was, the more people would travel it. Due to this, each kingdom took great care in maintaining its major trades routes and ensuring they were safe, which, in turn, influenced the amount of trade that entered the kingdom.

Another source of income for the monarchy was the taxes and tolls taken from the king's marketplace. The king's servant had a right to collect customary payments on each *iso* (trader's stall) on his behalf. The king could also collect taxes on special goods or demand payment or gifts on days of special occasions, like festivals. The king's wives could also receive gifts from traders whenever they visited the market, same with the palace servants.

The king also generated revenue by imposing taxes and levies on conquered towns and villages. These conquered towns and villages, known as *ereko*, would send tribute, gifts, and slaves to the kingdom now overseeing them. Although this practice varied from kingdom to kingdom, Oyo-Ile was the most known for using this practice. At the height of Oyo's glory, all of its *ereko* would send annual gifts and taxes, which were then used for the kingdom's development.

There were also traditions, rules, and customs that allowed the king to generate revenue. For instance, when the king settled a dispute between houses or lineages, both sides were required to send gifts to the king in appreciation. Also, some animals like leopards and elephants were regarded as royal property, so any hunter who succeeded in killing these animals must surrender them to the king. During a marriage or the funeral of a notable figure, part of the rites included sending gifts to the king. These gifts amounted to a substantial income for the ruler, thus making him richer than even the richest citizen.

The king also generated revenue from agriculture. In most kingdoms, kings had a large plot of land known as *oko oba,* meaning the "king's farmland," where his slaves and servants farmed produce for him daily. This farm was out of bounds from the general population, and produce from the farm was used to feed the king and his large household. Some of this produce was also taken to the market to sell. Other traders could only sell their produce of the same type once the king's produce had been sold.

Savings and Capital Formation

The emergence of more civilized kingdoms brought about a significant transformation in the manufacturing, commerce, and agricultural sectors. This induced changes in some economic activities like saving, although some forms of this practice already existed. The development of urban settlements brought about money-saving practices like the *ajo, esusu,* and other money-lending institutions.

The growth of the agricultural, commercial, and manufacturing sectors ensured an increase in the people's income. Also, major expenditures and family occasions like weddings and funerals led to the establishment of a savings system and other financial institutions. *Ajo*, meaning "gathering together," started with the development of urban Yoruba settlements. *Ajo* involved giving a contribution to a trustworthy person among a social group, whether it be an age group, traders' association, or agbo-ile. Each individual participating in *ajo* contributed the same amount of money at regular intervals to avoid confusion. Before an individual could collect his accumulated savings, he first needed to give the *alajo* (the one in charge of the savings) an advance notice.

There was one big problem with the *ajo* system: a low level of security. Often, the *alajo* was also a moneylender, which meant that he could loan out the money that had been deposited with him. If any loan went bad, his obligations to those saving with him would be disrupted. Usually, the people didn't get their money back, as the *alajo* would run away.

Another savings system that was practiced was the *esusu*, meaning "pooling and disbursing." With the *esusu*, each group member agreed upon a fixed sum to be paid at a specified time. The total amount of the money was paid to an individual in the group in rotation; thus, members of the group took turns collecting the total amount of money.

The *esusu* was well established in all parts of Yorubaland, with many *esusu* groups existing at once. The *esusu* had a president who oversaw the contributions and disbursement of money. The order in which the *esusu* would be disbursed was agreed upon before any contributions took place. Also, penalties and laws were stated before they started contributing. The lateness of any member in contributing was considered a serious offense. Any member expelled from the group had to wait until the end of the cycle when everyone had taken their share.

The *esusu* greatly aided low-income individuals in the early Yoruba kingdoms, and it still does. The *esusu* and *ajo* systems operated more like the banks we see today, and they are still impacting Yoruba communities to this day.

Loans and the Credit System

While the *ajo* and *esusu* systems offered loans, they were not available to the general public. This prompted the development of other types of loans and credit that were available to anyone. The first people to start handing out loans to the public were wealthy traders; however, others went fully into the trade and became moneylenders.

These moneylenders were known as *olowo-ele,* and they were providers of interest-bearing loans. These moneylenders did not necessarily have to accept payments of interest in cash; sometimes, they took payments in the form of goods, labor, or services. Another form of loans was the *iwofa,* but in this case, a person was given to serve the lender. Until the money was paid in full, the person had to serve the lender.

Another type of loan involved a farmer surrendering his farm. The lenders would then harvest it as a loan repayment. If anyone defaulted on the loan, the creditor could report the culprit to his lineage head. If that didn't work, the moneylender might employ the help of a distrainer. He would impose his presence on the debtor anytime and anyplace, giving the debtor no privacy. The distrainer was untouchable, as harming him meant violating the authority of the person who had employed him. Using a distrainer proved to be an effective method of recovering loans, as he attacked not only the debtor but also his lineage.

Oftentimes, to avoid the embarrassment and stigma that came from borrowing and defaulting on a loan, a compound usually came together to contribute the money or offer a satisfactory payment to the creditor.

The Impact of Women on the Economy

The Yorubas regarded some occupations as solely belonging to the male domain. For instance, women were exempted from tougher farm work. The women were assigned menial jobs and were more of a backup for the men. They cooked, fetched water, carried firewood, and did light harvesting. Although they were not heavily involved in the farm work, they were responsible for selling agricultural produce. Women were also heavily involved in crafts and the manufacturing processes; however, processes like metal smelting were still reserved for men. The Yoruba women were dominant in the kingdoms' commercial life. They created the trade network that shaped the Yoruba economy.

Chapter 6 – The Politics of the Early Yoruba Kingdoms

New cities and settlements were mostly created in two different ways. The first was through wars. Conflicts caused the destruction of pre-existing settlements and resulted in the victor merging their population with the original settlers, as seen with the founders of Ilesha and Owo. The other way was building upon existing infrastructure, like what Obanta and his people did in Ijebu-Ode, where they created structures typical of a Yoruba city, like the king's palace, king's marketplace, and the city walls. Awamaro did the same when founding Ado in Ekiti; he left the original settlers at the foot of the Olota Rock and continued building the city around the rock.

The populations in most Yoruba cities or towns were segmented; each segment or quarter had its own leaders, known as chiefs. This was especially true for the early settlers. The system of government in most Yoruba cities was a monarchial one since most of these kingdoms had their roots from Ile-Ife. Most of the migrants who left Ife to settle in a new place recreated the culture and traditions of their home kingdom wherever they settled.

The king's council was formed of chiefs from all the quarters of the city. The chief of the largest quarter was most likely the leader of the council, although leadership might have been based on other factors, such as ancestry, history, chivalry, and how famous or close they were to the king. Whenever a new group joined the city, the king's council met to decide the appropriate position for the new group leader. As the city grew, the king's council made recommendations to the king to create lower chieftaincy titles for the streets of each quarter, which would help the quarter chiefs.

The king's council, which usually only consisted of five or seven men, met with the king daily to make decisions concerning the kingdom; these decisions were then presented to the people as the king's decision. The council served as the highest court in the land, and it could only be overturned by the king. By law, the king could not make decisions without approval from the council. The council had different names, but it functioned roughly in the same manner in the different kingdoms. Other lower-level chiefs also met with the king, as his decisions were communicated to the chiefs for deliberation. If need be, they sent a message back to the king for modifications. When the king's decision was finalized, it was communicated through a town crier, who would go into the streets late in the evening and use a gong to garner attention before relaying the king's message. The chiefs would then see to it that the king's orders were carried out properly in their quarters.

The responsibility of selecting a new king fell mainly on the king's council. The throne was hereditary, but it was not always passed directly from father to son. All male members of the royal family, including sons and grandsons of former kings, were qualified to be king. Primogeniture was rejected in Yoruba culture to reduce the incidence of parricide among the crown princes. The crown prince, known as the Aremo, basically reigned alongside his father and performed royal duties. In the event of his father's death, the Aremo was expected to commit suicide. In 1858, Alaafin Atiba abolished the law, and he was succeeded by his son, Adelu, after his passing.

However, the Aremo still had to be elected by the council to become king. If he was found unworthy of such a position, he had to leave the city and live in a private residence in a satellite town of the kingdom. Though this course of action was not obligatory, it was usually inevitable since the new king's authority would supersede his own. He could also choose to die with his father.

The council's decision on who was to be king was final, and they viewed any agitation from competitors as a crime. Though the council members could be lobbied, they held themselves to a very high moral standard. After all, a high level of accountability and discipline was expected of them. No member of the council was allowed to take gifts from those seeking the title or even from members of the public.

Once a decision had been reached by the kingmakers, the person who was chosen was handed over to the right officials and priests for the coronation process to begin. The new king would live outside the palace in a compound for a few months, where he was instructed on how to behave and what to do and not to do before completing the necessary rituals. The kingmaker's council could also remove a king if they gauged his actions to be beyond the established controls of royal power; in other words, if he was immoral, greedy, or had tyrannical tendencies.

There were different methods of removing such a king from the throne. The council might give him an empty calabash (a type of gourd). Once the king opened it, he knew the council wanted him to commit suicide. He could also be given a dish of parrot eggs, which would have the same message as an empty calabash. The king also might be urged "to go to sleep" if it seemed he could not bear the burden of kingship. These methods of removal were performed to dignify the position of the king.

Prominent Wars and Treaties

The warlike nature of the Yoruba people is well known, so it is not surprising they were involved in many wars. With the slave trade thriving in the region, warlike individuals dominated. Still, many of the wars were fought at the behest of kings.

Gaha, an elite in the Oyo Empire during the 18th century, was named Bashorun (similar to a prime minister) in 1754. This event marked a turn for the worse in the history of the Oyo Empire. Gaha coveted the power and authorities of the Alaafin and deposed almost all the Alaafins he served under. Bashorun Gaha served five Alaafins; he influenced the death of four of them and tried to depose the fifth one (Alaafin Abiodun). However, he was unsuccessful in his last endeavor. This led to his death and the massacre of his family. Gaha was a great military leader and was beloved by his people for winning wars and protecting them from the tyranny of the Alaafins, but his own tyranny led to his downfall. His actions also kick-started the fall of the Oyo Empire.

After the death of Alaafin Abiodun of Oyo (r. c. 1770-1789), his son or cousin known as Awole (also spelled as Aole) was chosen as the new king. However, his reign was short and unhappy, which further contributed to the decline of the Oyo Empire.

According to custom, after Awole's coronation, the king sent out an expedition party to fight and destroy his enemies. During Awole's reign, which lasted from 1789 to 1796, he told the expedition party to eliminate the Baale (head of the clan) of Apomu, a town located in modern-day Ondo State.

This battle took place during a time when the slave trade was popular. Before Alaafin Abiodun had passed, he had agreed with both the Olowu of Owu and the Ooni of Ife to prevent the kidnapping and selling of their people; they, in turn, asked the Baale of Apomu to help prevent such events from happening again.

Awole traded along those routes with a friend. On one occasion, he decided to sell his friend, and it was reported to the Baale of Apomu that an Oyo man was being sold as a slave. The Baale of Apomu swooped in to arrest the individuals involved in this act of slavery. In the course of the investigation, it was discovered that Awole was the culprit. But since Awole was a prince, he could not be dealt with to the full extent of the law. The Baale didn't want judgment to be miscarried, so Awole was ordered to be flogged. Ever since then, Awole held a grudge, and this grudge manifested into actual conflict once he became king.

The Baale of Apomu ran to the Ooni of Ife to seek aid, but the Ooni could not save him. The Baale of Apomu committed suicide to appease the offended Alaafin and to prevent him from destroying his people. Regardless, according to tradition, an expedition had to be sent out, and Awole was asked who his enemies were. He replied, saying, "My enemies are too formidable." When further pressed to reveal his enemy, he named Afonja, a powerful chief. It is likely Awole named him because the Alaafin could see him being a potential source of trouble.

During this period, Afonja resided in Ilorin, an important military outpost in Oyo. Afonja held the title of Kakanfo, which is similar to a modern-day general. However, it took some maneuvering to get the title. After the former Kakanfo's death, Afonja demanded the title. But since he was a prince connected to the throne through his mother's side, the title was deemed to be beneath him. Eventually, the king granted Afonja's wish, as Afonja was a powerful individual who was willing to go to war for the title. Also, taking any action against Afonja would mean the outbreak of a civil war because many chiefs were loyal to him. Nevertheless, Afonja was added to Awole's list of enemies.

Eventually, though, other chiefs turned against Awole, namely Asamu the Bashorun. His quarrel with the Bashorun was over a Hausa trader who had lost his goods. This trader directly implored the king to help him get back his Koran, which was incredibly important to him. The king ordered the goods to be found and returned, but the Koran was not returned, although the trader did receive all of his other goods. The Hausa man pled for his priceless possession, and the king insisted the search must continue. The Bashorun, who knew where it was, refused to tell the king the truth. The king was deeply insulted by this, and he apparently said, "Has it come to this, that my commands cannot be obeyed in my capital? Must it be said that I failed to redress the grievance of a stranger in my town? That he appealed to me in vain?"

So, the king said to the Bashorun, "If you cannot find it, my father [the deity Shango, who was known for punishing thieves by burning the perpetrator's house] will find it for me." The next day, lightning struck the Bashorun's house, and the Bashorun was angry with the king for making him out to be a liar and a thief.

Another chief who was added to Awole's long list of enemies was Lafianu the Owota (believed to be a title of some kind). Lafianu had once protected Jankalawa, a man who had offended the late king and escaped to Bariba country (located in modern-day northeast Benin). After Alaafin Abiodun's death, Jankalawa returned, which annoyed the late king's wives. They complained and implored Awole to avenge this slight against the prior king.

After numerous appeals, Awole yielded and ordered the arrest and execution of Jankalawa. The Owota was angry for not being consulted, as the man had been under his protection. His ego was bruised since he had not been respected. So, the Bashorun, Kakanfo, and Owota became the king's enemies, and they conspired together.

The king was unwilling to confront the Kakanfo head-on, but he was advised by his counselors to send the Kakanfo to attack Iwere, a fortified city. Weapons were practically useless against the Iwere army. Back then, the Kakanfo's oath of office stated that he must either win within three months or die. Since Iwere was impregnable, he would more than likely have to commit suicide. The counselors decided not to warn the Kakanfo about this until he had been led to the foot of the hill where Iwere was built.

However, intelligence about the conspiracy reached the Kakanfo. Upon reaching the foot of the Iwere hill, Kakanfo attacked the royal party, which consisted of the king's brother, eunuchs, soldiers, and slaves, claiming that the king had set him and his army up for defeat by fighting an impregnable town.

Turning the army around, the Kakanfo, with the Bashorun and Owota at the head of the army, turned toward Oyo. The king sent word to inquire if the expedition was successful. The conspiring chiefs then sent word back, saying the royal party had insulted them and that the events that had unfolded had been unfortunate. The king asked them to come and personally inform him. However, the rebelling chiefs camped outside the capital and sent the king an empty calabash, a message telling him to commit suicide.

But before committing suicide, Awole took three arrows and an earthenware dish. He fired the arrows to the north, south, and west, uttering a curse upon the chiefs. Since they had been disloyal and disobedient to him, their children would be disobedient; when sent out on an errand, they would never return. Awole then broke the dish, which signified that the curse could not be reversed. After doing this, Awole took some poison and died. After pillaging the city and the palace, the chiefs and their forces disbanded. This ended an unhappy seven-year reign and began the nation's disintegration into tribal wars for independence.

The successor, Prince Adebo, became king at an unfortunate time, and he only spent 130 days on the throne. During this period, rebellion was the order of the day; he was essentially a king with no authority and power. Tributes were not sent to him, law and justice were subverted, and towns attacked each other to increase their wealth and power. Even the king's messengers no longer respected the ruler. Afonja the Kakanfo and Opele, the Baale of Gbogun, were the first to declare independence. Opele was the only chief Afonja respected, but he, unfortunately, died while fighting. Having no real rival, Afonja decided to pillage the towns and cities surrounding the capital to isolate it. In around 1817, to further strengthen his position, Afonja invited a Muslim priest named Alimi to Ilorin to serve as his personal priest. Alimi accepted the position and also brought some Hausa slaves, whom Afonja deployed as soldiers. Afonja also invited a rich friend named Solagberu, who could potentially help finance the war effort.

Ojo Agunbambaru was one of Bashorun Gaha's children who had survived the massacre; he escaped to Bariba country. After becoming aware of the happenings in the state, he decided to come back and exploit the opportunity to avenge his father and get a title for himself. He brought a large army from Bariba and killed chiefs who were friends or allies with Afonja, doing so under the pretext of avenging the king.

In total, it is thought that Ojo killed more than one hundred chiefs who could oppose him, with Lafianu the Owota being his first victim. After taking over Oyo, Ojo set a course for Ilorin to fight Afonja. Ojo's campaign did not enjoy the support of other chiefs due to the indiscriminate killings of rulers. If Ojo had not killed so many chiefs, it is possible that they might have pitied his plight and joined him in going to war against Afonja, as he was only growing stronger as time passed.

Ojo also threatened Adegun, the Onikoyi of Ikoyi-Ile, who could have been a great addition to his camp. Ikoyi-Ile was located ten miles from Oyo, and it was founded by a different Adegun, one of Oduduwa's descendants.

Ojo's army wreaked so much destruction that towns deserted as it approached. The Oyo people following him did so out of fear, not out of loyalty. The Onikoyi, Afonja's friend, even secretly joined Ojo's ranks, keeping Afonja abreast of Ojo's policies and movements. The Oyo people and the Onikoyi hatched a plan to desert Ojo during the heat of battle.

Afonja met Ojo's army far from Ilorin, and a battle ensued. Afonja was defeated in three engagements, costing him most of his soldiers. Afonja fled back to Ilorin to fortify the city's defenses with stockades made from shea and locust trees since Ilorin had no walls.

The Onikoyi and his men besieged Ilorin, and Afonja had a hard time beating the attackers back. The Onikoyi sent a message to Afonja to persevere a bit longer. Right when the city was about to fall, the Onikoyi and his men retreated, leaving Ojo behind, who lost the battle. Ojo was deserted by those he thought he was fighting for. Somehow, he managed to escape death, and he retreated back to Bariba country.

The Battle of Ogele (1824–1825)

In 1823/24, Afonja was killed by the Hausa Jamas (enlisted soldiers). They had been ordered to do so by Alimi, Afonja's priest. This shocked and bewildered everyone since Afonja had been the Kakanfo. It also threw the Yoruba nation into disarray. A conclave was called to unite and avenge his death, not knowing that Alimi, who was now controlling Ilorin, had prepared for the conflict. (This was how Islam took hold in Ilorin, as many Yoruba Muslim clerics started to emerge. From here on, the religion began to spread through the clerics until it became popular among the commoners and the people in the Yoruba palaces.)

Alimi had studied the Yorubas for a long time and understood how to defeat them. Toyeje, the Baale of Ogbomoso (a town close to Oyo-Ile), was elevated to the position of Kakanfo, and he united the whole nation to chase the Fulanis out of Ilorin. (The Fulanis remain one of the largest ethnic groups in West Africa, and they are primarily Muslim.) Toyeje and his men decided to camp in Ogele, located in the Edo region. There, they fought the Fulanis, who were led by Solagberu, Afonja's rich friend.

The Fulanis were victorious in this bloody battle, which led to the destruction of many towns. The Fulanis pursued the Yorubas vigorously, so the refugees only had a limited amount of time to choose a few of their personal things to take or else risk being captured. Children went missing, and older people were sometimes left behind. The people were bereft of money and items of value, reducing them to a life of poverty and misery. Thus, the Yorubas' first attempt to retrieve Ilorin resulted in a sound defeat for them.

The Mugbamugba War (1824–1825)

After a brief period of rest, the Yorubas decided to rally together again. This time, they were determined to chase the Fulanis and the Hausa Jamas out of Ilorin. The Yorubas allied with the king of Rabbah (believed to be the Nupe king, possibly Majiya II). The war commenced sometime between March and April.

Many towns and villages were already devasted from the previous war, so by the time the second war erupted, the country was on the brink of famine. Since farmlands were not tended to because of the previous war, the Yorubas and the Fulanis devoured the food they found on Ilorin farms, and when nothing was left, they started eating locust fruit (*igba*)— hence the name "Mugbamugba." (*Mu* in Yoruba means to take, drink, or bring something. Thus, *mu igba* (put together as "mugba") would mean to take locust fruit.)

The Fulanis and their calvary triumphed against the Yorubas because they did not understand how to defeat the Fulani horsemen, causing them to lose courage and strength. During the battle, the Fulanis employed a new tactic in which they left their main cavalry at the rear of the Yorubas and attacked with a few horsemen during the heat of battle. This allowed the cavalry to quickly attack from the rear and destroy the Yorubas.

The Fulanis triumphed easily with their horses in open fields, and when the Yorubas fled to fortified towns, they only found famine, which was further exacerbated by the ensuing siege. The king escaped to Rabbah, leaving the Yorubas at the mercy of the Fulanis, who were now emboldened with the taste of victory. They decided to pillage all of the towns in the direction of Ofa, Erin, and Igbona, with their inhabitants and kings escaping to Ikoyi.

The Battle of Pamo (1825-1831)

Ilorin was eventually delivered into the hands of the Fulanis. After the death of Alimi (the sources are unclear of when this actually happened, which is a problem that plagues much of Yoruba history), he was succeeded by Abdulsalami, his son, who became the first Emir of Ilorin, solidifying the family's claim to Ilorin. To better understand the family's desire to claim Ilorin, we have to go back and look at Alimi's history in the city. During Afonja's reign, Alimi had been greatly displeased with Afonja's excesses and wanted to leave. He had never intended to stay for long in the first place, but he was begged to stay in the city by the Yoruba leaders. They wanted someone to keep Afonja's ambitions in check, and they greatly respected the Muslim priest.

So, he sent for his wife, who was apparently barren. His wife consulted with another Muslim priest about her barrenness, and she was told to give a slave as alms to a distinguished Muslim priest. The greatest priest she knew was her own husband, so she gave one of her female slaves to Alimi. This slave gave birth to Alimi's two eldest sons: Abdulsalami and Shitta. Alimi's wife also became pregnant, and she gave birth to another son whom they named Sumonu (also known as Beribepo). Alimi married again, and this wife gave birth to yet another son. Together, these four sons would inherit Alimi's properties after his death.

Abdulsalami and his full-blooded brother took over the city, leaving nothing to the first wife's son. It is unknown if the fourth son received anything; it is possible that he had died by this time. With the brothers' newfound power, they decided to conquer Yorubaland. They played unsuspecting Yoruba leaders against each other. These leaders were jealous of each other's strength, fame, and military conquests, and their antagonistic and petty feelings led to many defeats among the Yoruba chiefs, who stood no chance without being united.

So, Kakanfo Toyeje quarreled with Onikoyi Adegun, which led to war. To strengthen his position, the Kakanfo formed a league with the Timi of Ede, Solagberu of Ilorin, and the Oluiwo of Iwo to besiege Ikoyi. Solagberu already had a personal vendetta against Adegun for not paying him the proper homage.

The allied forces camped in the city of Pamo, and from there, they fought against the people of Ikoyi, almost subduing the city. A refugee living in the city actually saved the day by asking the Onikoyi if he could be allowed to use his wisdom to save the city. The Onikoyi was tired of the war and looking for a peaceful settlement, so this request was granted. The refugee decided to send a private messenger to Abdulsalami in the Onikoyi's name, saying he pledged allegiance to the Emir of Ilorin. Upon hearing this, the Emir told Solagberu to withdraw, but he refused.

After successive orders with the same outcome, Abdulsalami asked the chiefs, princes, and any loyal personnel to immediately return home, leaving Solagberu alone. In order to raise the siege, the Emir sent out another force to reinforce Ikoyi. But after reaching Ikoyi, the Ilorin soldiers drank themselves to a stupor for ten days. On the eleventh day, they joined forces with the Onikoyi. They defeated Kakanfo Toyeje's army, leaving great men dead on the battlefield.

Solagberu fled back to Ilorin. Although he was allowed to stay there, Solagberu greatly resented the Emir, a feeling that was reciprocated. Every incident in the city seemed to increase the tensions between the two men until it led to war. The Emir besieged Okesuna, where Solagberu was residing. Eventually, the people at Okesuna had to face facts, as they were all suffering from famine. In the end, Solagberu was killed.

Abdulsalami was now without a major opponent. The Onikoyi had pledged allegiance to him, and the Kakanfo's army was destroyed. Thus, Abdulsalami decided to declare himself the king of Yorubaland. The rest of the Yoruba towns were made to give tribute. Abdulsalami used his Jamas to help with this, and they ended up oppressing the people, taking their livestock, wives, and children whenever they chose to.

The Owu War

With the Fulanis victorious and most of the kingdoms in disarray, each state claimed independence and sovereignty and fought for its own interest. The people of Ijebu and Ife toward the south and east, respectively, allied together against the Owus.

The Owu people were known for their stubbornness, immorality, hardiness, and arrogance. Although the Owus' mannerisms were different from the Oyos, they always stood by the Alaafin. The Owu people were also great warriors, with their weapons of choice being the cutlass and the bow and arrow.

The war between the Owus and Oyos started during the reign of King Abiodun, who gave an order saying that the Oyo people must not be kidnapped and sold at Apomu. In around 1821, a similar order came from Onikoyi Adegun and Kakanfo Toyeje. When their armies carried out these orders, they ended up destroying several towns, all of which were Ife territories.

The Ooni of Ife was greatly displeased by this, and he declared war on Owu, entrusting the command to Singunsin. The party camped at the confluence of the Osun and Oba Rivers in a farm village called

Dariagbon.

The Ife considered themselves to be very brave and warlike, so they thought victory would be easy. However, the Owus, upon hearing the news of the war, immediately set out to engage their enemies, whom they annihilated. The few Ifes who lived to tell the tale escaped to Iwo, but fearing reprisal from the Owus, the king of Iwo told the Ifes they could not stay. However, he sympathized so much with their cause that he allowed them to gather their forces together and prepare for another attack in Adunbieiye, which was nearby. The Ifes remained there for around five years due to both shame and the lack of reinforcements.

In the meantime, the Owus arrogant nature caused another incident; they destroyed Apomu over a trading dispute with Ijebu. This resulted in the death of many Ijebus.

The king of Iwo advised the Ifes and Ijebus to ally against the Owus. The Ifes reinforced their forgotten army in Adunbieiye, and the Ijebus, being closer to the coast, had access to guns from the Europeans and were well-armed. The Owus heard about the war and rushed out with cutlass in hand to meet the Ijebus. However, their weapons were no match for the Ijebus' guns, and the Owus incurred heavy losses.

After regrouping, the Owus engaged the Ijebus again, suffering yet another loss. The Owus retreated a short distance away, where they regrouped and engaged the Ijebus once more. They were again defeated. With their courage broken and resigned to their fate, they retreated to Owu to fortify their city for the siege they knew was coming.

The Ijebus and Ifes encamped under a tree known as the Ogungun. They engaged the Owus, who defended their town against the siege for years (some historians say five years, while others say seven). But even though the people fought bravely, famine could not be avoided. The Owus ate large beans called *popondo* or *awuje*, which were thought to be unfit to eat as food.

The allied forces could neither crush the wall nor destroy the gate. Eventually, the Olowu opened a gate and escaped to Erunmu, one of the towns under Owu rule. The chief of Erunmu, though related to the Ooni of Ife, protected the Olowu. After the fall of Owu, the chief of Erunmu was pardoned for assisting the Owu ruler.

After the conquest of Owu, the allies returned to their camp by the Ogungun tree. There, they agreed that Owu should never be rebuilt. Oje, the closest town to Owu, could not expand beyond the Ogungun tree. The Owu land was still cultivated, but no building was placed on its soil. In 1873, someone built a farmhouse on Owu land. The home was immediately ordered to be destroyed, and the man was fined for putting it up. So, Owu remains unbuilt, with its ancient structures abandoned. However, people are living around the ruins, and many Owu descendants moved to Abeokuta, which is located in present-day Ogun State, Nigeria.

This war on Owu contains a historical first, as it was the first time gunpowder weapons were used by the Yorubas to fight. The war also laid the foundation for the destruction of other Egba towns and the creation of modern-day Abeokuta and Ibadan, the latter of which is located in present-day Oyo State, Nigeria. Ibadan is also the largest capital city in Nigeria in terms of geographical area.

Chapter 7 – The Rise and Fall of the Oyo Empire

The history of Yorubaland is not complete without mentioning the great Oyo Empire. The early Oyo Empire consisted of parts of what is currently western Nigeria and the eastern Republic of Benin. The ancient Oyo Empire was founded around the mid-7th century, and it rose to prominence as the largest West African empire by the 18th century, surpassing even Ife. This was due to the efforts of their kings, known as Alaafins. From its creation by Oranyan to the present day, it has grown to become the biggest Yoruba-speaking state, and it has political influence over a large portion of other Yorubaland kingdoms.

However, the early Oyo Kingdom, when compared to its other early counterparts such as Owu and Ila, was smaller in size and military might. It was essentially seen as the younger brother to the other Yoruba kingdoms. One of the reasons for this is that it was created after the major Yoruba kingdoms had become established.

But by the 17th century, the Oyo Empire had become stronger and wealthier, and it had a larger landmass. The capital of this blossoming empire was known as Oyo-Ile. However, it was known to their Hausa neighbors as Oyo Katunga. This new empire was comprised of several Yoruba-speaking peoples and non-Yoruba speaking peoples, like the Nupe, Bariba, and Aja. The kingdom also expanded westward as far as the Aja country in Benin and part of the Ashanti Empire in the modern-day Republic of Togo.

The Oyo Empire at its greatest extent

The Oyo Empire experienced a few setbacks during its journey to becoming a great power, but it became prominent through wealth gotten from trade with other neighboring kingdoms and Europeans. And with its powerful cavalry, they were able to dominate and conquer other African states.

The Rise of the Oyo Empire

In previous chapters, we talked about the first three kings of the Oyo Empire: Ajaka, Shango, and Aganju. You also might recall Oranyan, but it is important to note that he was not regarded as the first Alaafin despite founding the Oyo Empire. Instead, he was simply known as Oba Oranyan. There were many rulers of Oyo, such as Oluaso, who is said to have had 1,460 children, but only the most influential will be discussed below.

Ongibogi (r. c. 1500–c. 1537)

During his reign, the Oyo capital was besieged by the Nupe king. Around 1535, the Nupes occupied the capital, and many of the Oyos fled to Borgu, which was located in northwestern Nigeria.

Eguguoju (ruled during the 16ᵗʰ century)

Eguguoju became the leader of the Oyo people while they were still in exile. The prior king, Onifran, had hoped to retake Oyo from the Nupe, and Eguguoju had the same dream. He and his followers camped in a forest on their way to Oyo. While Eguguoju was sitting at the foot of a tree, two birds, Igbo and Oyo, chased after each other from the top of the tree to the ground where Eguguoju was. He ordered that the birds be killed. This incident made him determined to fight to his last breath to regain Oyo.

When they reached Oyo, there was a ferocious battle against the Nupes. Eguguoju ended up moving the capital to Oyo Igboho ("New Oyo"). Some say that he named the capital after the birds who had inspired him to fight.

Orompoto (r. c. 1554–c. 1562)

Orompoto was Eguguoju's sister, and she was the first woman to be the king of Oyo in the era of imperialism. She became the king because there was no male successor to take control of Oyo. According to some traditions, she transformed into a man before assuming the throne. She was a skilled warrior on horseback, and she drove the Nupes away from the capital in 1555. She also apparently displayed her bravery in the Battle of Ilayi.

In the battle, three of her war chiefs died. The last one fell on the ground, a grin still on his face. He looked as if he was still alive, so the Oyos' enemies thought that the chiefs were impossible to beat, and they fled the battlefield.

Ajiboyede (ruled sometime during the 16th century)

Ajiboyede was the next Alaafin of Oyo. Early on in his reign, the Nupes again attacked the empire. Victory was on the side of the Nupe warriors until Ajanlapa, a court official, took a daring tactic. Ajanlapa told Ajiboyede to give him his crown and clothes to wear. Ajiboyede did this, and Ajanlapa ran toward the Nupes, making them think that he was the king. They shot arrows at him, and eventually, one fatally pierced him. The Nupes were wrong in thinking they had won, though; Ajanlapa's men quickly attacked the Nupe warriors and killed them.

Ajiboyede celebrated a festival called Bebe, which celebrated the defeat of the Nupes. The festival was held for many years after, and it gave the people the chance to take joy in the peace that now enveloped the empire. Due to this peace, commerce and agriculture began to boom, and the new capital of Igboho grew. As a result of this, two major markets were established, and the city became known for its acquisition of horses from Hausaland, located in sub-Saharan Africa.

Abipa (ruled late 16th to early 17th century)

Abipa was the next Alaafin, and he was the son of Eguguoju. He wanted to fulfill his father's last request of taking the seat of government back to Oyo. However, apparently, not everyone agreed with this move. Abipa refused to listen to them, so they planned to do something to change his decision. When Abipa's scouting party reached Oyo-Ile, people came out at night with torches and roamed about the place. The scouts believed they were spirits that disapproved of moving the seat of government.

This devastated the king, and he didn't know what to do. However, he thought that something was up, so he sent some hunters to investigate the matter. They found out that they were not spirits but rather human beings. One of the hunters attempted to shoot one of the humans but changed his mind when the man begged to be spared.

There is a story that says the men who masqueraded as ghosts were taken before the king. The king's nobles acted as if they knew nothing about this, even though some of them definitely did. The king decided to hold this close to his chest until the court gathered for the Jakuta sacrifices, which were made to Shango. After they were done with the proceedings, they advanced to the banquet hall to dine. However, the usual servants didn't present the food and drinks. Instead, the men who had played ghosts were the ones who came out to serve them.

The noblemen were surprised, and everyone ate quietly. They parted without a farewell to the king. Those involved in the plot showed no remorse for what they did. Instead, they poisoned the king's adviser.

The seat of government was finally moved to Oyo-Ile. Abipa buried charms in different places so that the capital of Oyo would never be destroyed by war. A medicine man asked for a newborn baby to be used as the ingredient for the charm. At that time, Abipa's wife had just given birth, so he ordered that the baby be killed. Then he handed the dead baby to the medicine man to do with as he wished. This act won the hearts of many because they understood how difficult it was for Abipa to sacrifice his son for them.

After this incident, Oyo-Ile was never destroyed by war.

Obalokun (ruled during the 17th century)

Obalokun's reign was a short one, but some interesting things happened during it. For instance, salt was first introduced into Yorubaland during his rule. Also, Obalokun was in direct communication with the king of France, and supposedly, both of them were friends. He sent eight hundred messengers to take presents to France, but he never heard of them again.

Other Events during the Oyo Empire's Rise

With its rearing expansion, the empire attempted to attack the Benin Empire between 1578 and 1608 (most likely during Abipa's reign or at least partly during his reign). Although their efforts failed at first, they eventually conquered the Benin Empire and made them pay tribute to Oyo. The Oyo Empire developed an efficient system of collecting tributes and sending them back to the capital. This system was executed through representatives, known as Ajele, who were sent to govern the conquered communities. The Ajele were controlled and kept in check by the royal messengers known as the Ilari. All of this was backed up by an efficient military that was personally controlled by the Alaafin.

The efficient organization of the Oyo Empire in managing its conquered regions and communities boosted its rise. These regions were seen as being part of a larger entity. Since the empire had roots connecting them to Ile-Ife, its influence also spread to southern Yorubaland.

The areas under the control of the Oyo Empire can be divided into four main parts: metropolitan Oyo, where the capital was situated; Yorubaland; Ajaland, which was near the Kingdom of Benin; and the

Egbado Corridor, located southwest of Yorubaland. All of these states practiced the same system of government, which was dictated by the capital of Oyo, making them a well-oiled machine for easy control by the Alaafin and his representatives.

Aside from its military advantage, the Oyo Empire's geographical location made it an important trading route, connecting many regional locations. They were also able to control and direct the volume of trade with the Hausa and people from Gao and Timbuktu. Significant amounts of Oyo textiles and iron products were sent to these regions in exchange for horses. These horses were used mainly for military purposes. The Oyos also controlled the slave trade to other West African states and kingdoms. This control over trading made the Oyo Empire extremely wealthy, and it significantly accelerated the development of the empire, both economically and militarily.

Factors That Contributed to the Rise of the Oyo Empire

A lot of factors helped shape Oyo into a military and economic powerhouse. One factor that helped this tiny kingdom initially was the adversity and destruction it faced from its neighbors. This might sound like the opposite of helping, but it played a major role in how Oyo developed.

The capital's location made it a prime target for the Nupes and the Bariba people of Borgu from the northeast and northwest, respectively. These kingdoms were already well established in the region. They did not specifically target only Oyo-Ile, as they also attacked other Yoruba kingdoms as well.

This leads into yet another factor that aided in the development of Oyo, with both factors going hand in hand with each other. This second factor was the location of their capital: Oyo-Ile. The kingdom was located along one of the oldest trade routes, and it connected the forests and grasslands of central West Africa to the middle Niger. This made it a desirable spot for any ambitious kingdom. The new capital was attacked and threatened so much that it paid a lot of tribute to the Nupe and Bariba people in the north and the Owu Kingdom in the south. Although the Oyos lost Oyo-Ile, they eventually got it back, and they chased away their enemies.

The Oyo people knew they had to change their ways in order to survive and put a stop to all these attacks. So, the Oyos learned extensively from their neighbors by examining their efficient centralized system of government and strong military. The Oyos now knew they had to establish a military that would subdue and deter any attacks on them. Unlike other Yoruba kingdoms, Oyo-Ile overcame these problems and eventually became a recognized empire with military and economic strength.

Also, the location of Oyo-Ile provided a defensive cover that prevented its enemies from attacking it. It was located in a spot where natural barriers made it almost impregnable to outside forces. The range of rocky hills surrounding the city made the maneuverability of enemy forces difficult, making the city less accessible for a direct attack. Asides from this natural barrier, the people built great walls around the city, and for nearly two centuries, no enemy came directly to the capital.

Agriculture was another factor that greatly assisted in the rise of the Oyo Empire. The city was situated in a region favorable for growing crops. The savannah grassland and its low rolling hills provided fertile soil for crops. Also, the region possessed streams that served as a good water source, with the Osun River flowing from the south and the Niger River coming from the north.

Farming on a larger scale allowed for a rapid increase in the population of the capital, which leads us to the next factor: a rise in the population. By the late 15th century, the Oyo cities were easily the most populated cities in Yorubaland; this allowed for the easy recruitment of men, and it ultimately helped build their military into an all-conquering army.

In addition to farming, another advantage provided by the savannah grassland was the use of horses, which they received from trading with the Hausas in the north. Horses allowed for easier communication and transportation over long distances. This also became a military advantage, and it helped the growing kingdom subdue its neighbors.

Horses aided in establishing administrative and commercial actions that could have been a nightmare for such a large empire. It also enabled them to conquer and control lands that were far from the capital. Oyo officials were often aware of the happenings in distant areas.

The control of commerce in the region also played into the hands of the Oyo people since their capital was established along important and well-known trade routes. The Oyos dominated the trading world compared to other kingdoms during its peak in the 18th century. They traded embroidery with the Hausas in the north in exchange for horses. Furthermore, they traded iron tools with Ajaland in the south. They were also heavily involved in the slave trade and were one of the first kingdoms to trade slaves with the Europeans. The large volume of trade controlled by the empire brought enormous wealth to the empire and its people.

Another contributing factor to the rise of the Oyo Empire was the general acceptance and support it had from other Yoruba kingdoms. Kingdoms like Owu and Ila suffered from raids and attacks from the Nupes and Bariba people as well, and they saw the breakthrough of Oyo as more of a success than as another source of competition. The Alaafin was part of the Yoruba kingship family who came from Ile-Ife, so his success and influence were seen as that of an influential member and as something not to be feared but embraced.

At the height of the Oyo Empire's power, the Alaafin even acted as an intermediary in disputes between other Yoruba kingdoms. These kingdoms offered support, hospitality, and supplies to Oyo soldiers conducting military campaigns in far-away regions. One good example is

Ila, where their king provided aid to Oyo troops while fighting against the Nupe people. Oyo reciprocated by allowing easy trade and travel into its territories. This close relationship with other Yoruba kingdoms bolstered the Alaafin's influence. All of these factors aided in the military, economic, and political rise of the Oyo Empire.

Political Life in the Oyo Empire

During the glory days of the Oyo Empire, the political situation ensured that prosperity was certain. Unlike most of the other Yoruba kingdoms, the Oyo people developed a sophisticated political structure that ensured checks and balances for a smooth transition of power and eliminated abuse by the Alaafin. This helped them to govern their conquered domains effectively.

The typical Yoruba system of government was employed in the Oyo Empire, with the head being the Alaafin. The Alaafin was chosen from a pool of princes who were descended from Oranyan. However, the first son of the king was not included in this pool. If you can call recall, the first son was known as the Aremo, and he had to die by committing suicide when his father died. This was because succession by primogeniture was largely rejected by the Yoruba kingdoms. This practice was later abandoned.

The kingmakers, known as the Oyo Mesi, were established to enthrone a king and also dethrone him by giving him an empty calabash or a dish of parrot eggs, thereby forcing him to commit suicide. (It should be noted that the Oyo Mesi is still around today, but it takes more of a ceremonial role.) The Oyo Mesi were seven councilors, consisting of the Agbaakin, the Samu, the Alapini, the Laguna, the Akiniku, and the Ashipa. They were all led by the Bashorun. They acted like politicians with electoral and legislative powers, which prevented the Alaafin from being an absolute ruler with infinite power. Each councilor had a specific duty to perform at court each day.

While the chiefs that made up the Oyo Mesi might not have been from the royal bloodline, they assisted the Alaafin in governing the kingdom. They made decisions and laws for the good of the kingdom. In civic ceremonies, the Alaafin had the power of life and death over his subjects, but in reality, the ruler was subject to the Oyo Mesi.

In line with the empire's military policy, the Oyo Mesi were also military chiefs. The officer presiding over the Oyo Mesi was the Bashorun, who held the highest office among the council. His responsibility was akin to that of a prime minister, and he controlled the army. The Laguna acted more in an ambassadorial role for the empire. The Alapini was in charge of the religious affairs of the state, especially the Egungun festival and the Ifa cult. These festivals and practices were the accepted state religion.

In choosing a king, the Bashorun had to consult the Ifa oracle before selecting a new Alaafin, who generally came from one of the three royal houses. Although the position of the king was not necessarily hereditary, the successors still had to be a descendant of Oranyan.

As powerful as the Oyo Mesi may appear, their power was also checked. The Ogboni might not have had any political or administrative authority, but it was backed by religion. Since the group primarily consisted of old sages noted for their knowledge in religious and political affairs, it was highly regarded by the people, so it was able to influence the Oyo Mesi's decisions and have direct access to the Alaafin on matters of the state.

Though the military was controlled by the Alaafin, it was still involved in checking the control of powerful individuals. Soldiers could be used to compel and dissuade a tyrannical Alaafin or even the Oyo Mesi into changing their opinions about matters of state.

Palace affairs were controlled by many high- and low-ranked officials that numbered up to a hundred. These officials attended to the king's needs and that of his family as well. They also tended to the palace and ensured daily rituals were done properly. Eunuchs, whose presence was uncommon in other Yoruba cultures, attended to the king's wives and children.

Outside the empire's capital of Oyo-Ile, the other conquered regions were governed by individuals appointed by the Alaafin. They served as his representative in the region and carried out his instructions. These conquered regions were supposed to serve the capital by providing goods, services, humans, and material resources. At the peak of its power, the Oyo Empire was comprised of many tributary states.

The Notorious Alaafins of the Oyo Empire

Although it seems like most of the rulers of Oyo looked out for the interests of the people, that was certainly not the case. Some rulers were tyrants who pushed the envelope on what they could do to demonstrate their power. We have selected three rulers of Oyo and included the various legends surrounding their reign. It might seem that these men brought about the decline of the empire, but that was not the case. You will notice that all of them ended up either dying in battles to retain their power or committing ritual suicide, as the people held their kings to a higher standard.

Karan

The dates of Karan's reign are not known, but he succeeded Odarawu, who ruled during the late 17th century. He was a tyrant and the worst of them all. He was so cruel to his subjects that his name was attached to a saying: "as cruel as Karan."

A conspiracy began when he sent an expedition to Aga Oibo. At some point, the people on the expedition had rebellious thoughts and were ready for action. It was made known to them by divination that Karan couldn't be conquered unless they offered his fan-bearer as a sacrifice to the gods. They sent a message to him requesting his fan-bearer, and he agreed.

After they sacrificed the fan-bearer to the gods, they sent back meat. Karan ate it, and they declared that Karan's words no longer had value since he had just eaten his servant. Hence, his army would no longer be charged with disobedience if they decided to go against him.

Karan's death was demanded, but he didn't want to go down without a fight. Even though the whole army was against him, he shot arrows at them until his hands were swollen. He climbed to the top of the roof to continue shooting, but the people burned the palace. He died in the fire.

Jayin

Jayin was next in line, and he was the son of Alaafin Karan. He wasn't much different from his tyrannical father. Olusi, his son, had a tender and caring personality. Everyone depended on Olusi to give the country a better future, but he fell under the charms of one of his father's wives. His father was already jealous of Olusi's popularity, and once this happened, Jayin decided he had to take drastic actions.

One version explained that while his father reprimanded him, Jayin had a club in his hand, and the top of the club was spiked with poison. He drove the club into Olusi's head, and Olusi didn't survive.

Another version says Olusi was given poisoned bean cakes by his father, which killed him. Either way, Olusi died because his father poisoned him.

Olusi was gravely mourned, and the chiefs wanted to find out who was behind his death because they couldn't believe Jayin's story that his son's death was due to a kick from his horse. The truth was eventually spilled by one of the wives, and this made the chiefs hate the king.

Apparently, chanters approached the palace. Jayin heard them, and he thought it was best to kill himself before the chanters began incorporating his cruel act into their songs.

Ayibi (ruled during the 17th century)

Ayibi was crowned when he was old enough. However, he disappointed his people because he had no respect for them and took pleasure in shedding blood. Whenever a case was brought to him, he always ordered the execution of both the complainant and the defendant. He never respected anyone, even those older than him in age and rank.

One day, he was with his wife in the bath when she made a statement. "And this is all of the man dreaded by all." He didn't like what she had said, but he covered his displeasure with a smile. After he left the bathroom, he privately told an executioner to fetch the head of his wife's mother and father and place them in calabashes.

The executioner did this and brought the calabashes to him. Ayibi sent for his wife and told her to open them. She did so, and he asked her if she knew them. With tears in her eyes, she said she knew them. Then he said, "That is the reason I am so much dreaded by all, although to you I am commonplace and ordinary." She expected him to kill her, but he disappointed her. Instead, he loved the misery he saw in her eyes.

His cruelty made the city reject him, and because of this, he committed suicide.

It might not make much sense to people today that people as dreaded as Ayibi, Jayin, and Shango committed suicide. But the reason almost all rejected kings committed suicide was that anyone who was proclaimed as king was sacred and venerated by the gods. The moment his followers spoke the words "We reject you," he must die by his own hands. This was because a king could not return to being a private individual or continue ruling after making his followers suffer.

The people would prefer not to kill the Alaafin because he was sacred; instead, he had to kill himself. If the king killed himself, he would have an honorable burial. But if he didn't, and the people eventually killed him, his corpse would be treated like garbage, and his house would be pulled down. Hence, most of them decide to commit suicide for the sake of their relatives.

The Fall of the Oyo Empire

The Oyo Empire served as a representative measure for the other Yoruba kingdoms since it was the largest and most dominant for centuries. It could also be said that its fall from grace affected the other Yoruba kingdoms too. The decline of this glorious empire began in early 1754 when the power-hungry Bashorun, Gaha, started a coup that led to the empire's demise. He conspired with the other Oyo Mesi and the Ogboni to remove four successive Alaafins from the throne by forcing them to commit suicide. They presented all of them with a calabash containing parrot eggs.

Bashorun Gaha's hold on the throne was only broken during the reign of Alaafin Abiodun. In 1774, Abiodun executed Gaha due to his constant plotting and scheming. However, the cracks brought about during the tumultuous reign of Gaha never really closed; rather, they widened, which ultimately led to the collapse of the Oyo Empire.

After overcoming Bashorun Gaha, Alaafin Abiodun conducted raids against Borgu (home of the Bariba). They all failed, which led to a decline in the Alaafin's popularity. After Abiodun's death, his son or cousin, Awole, assumed the throne. These events begin a chain of cataclysmic actions, starting with the breakaway of Ilorin led by Kakanfo Afonja.

What happened next was described in the prior chapter, but eventually, Awole committed suicide. After Awole's death, Oyo declined into civil war, with numerous factions fighting for the throne. With a weakened Oyo Mesi, this civil war escalated, and for almost twenty years, the factions could not agree on a new Alaafin. This power tussle created a huge vacuum in a capital already filled with powerful military commanders. It also led to the separation of Ilorin from Oyo in 1817. Ilorin did not remain independent for long, though. Alimi killed Afonja, and in 1823, Ilorin became part of the Sokoto Caliphate, which had been founded in 1804 during the Fulani Wars.

By 1825, the Oyo Empire was a shadow of its former self. Alaafin Majotu (r. 1802–1830) sought the help of the British and the Oba of Benin in putting down the rebellions caused by Ilorin. Part of the problem was that the Oyos no longer had full access to their soldiers, as many of them, as well as horses, had been stationed in Ilorin, which was now under the control of the Muslims. The Alaafin was also made to convert to Islam.

Ilorin destroyed many Oyo villages in its attempt to take over the empire. Eventually, the Muslims reached the capital of Oyo-Ile and destroyed it in 1835. The destruction of Oyo-Ile by the Fulanis led to the capital being moved south to Ago d'Oyo. This action led to a shift in power to Ibadan, which was already a settlement for war generals. This action would be the straw that broke the camel's back. The Oyo Empire never regained its authority and importance in Yorubaland. In 1888, Oyo became one of Great Britain's protectorates.

It was easy for Britain to gain access to Yorubaland due to the role it played during the slave trade. Europeans, such as Hugh Clapperton, who were interested in legitimate trade after the abolishment of the slave trade in 1807, toured Yorubaland and Hausaland. The exploration of the regions laid the path for British colonization.

In 1914, while Oyo was under colonial rule, the Province of Oyo was created, and it constituted Oyo, Ilesha, Ife, and Ila. Oyo Province was surrounded by Ilorin to the north; Abeokuta, Ijebu-Ode, and Ondo to the south; Dahomey to the west; and Kontagora to the east. The monarchs of the four Oyo Province kingdoms continued ruling.

Colonization facilitated the improvement of trade, sanitization, and the development of better structures. Schools, pharmacies, town halls, hospitals, and post offices were built. With advanced knowledge of architecture and modifications to suit the weather from the British, new residential structures were put in place.

The first native school was introduced in 1928. The British colonizers focused on advancing the "primitive but progressive" Yorubas in terms of science, language, and religion. British teachers were present to teach the English language. Christian missionaries were also present in the schools to convert the young children to the new religion, and they were taught to pass the message to their parents. Christianity was fiercely resisted by the elders in the communities, as the religion went against their traditional practices and ways of living. But as Western ideas of rationalism and individualism became more pronounced among the educated, they began to replace the traditional teachings, allowing Christianity to take hold.

Chapter 8 – Folklore Stories

Yoruba folk tales were passed down through the generations. It was an effective way of not forgetting the customs, as well as imbibing moral lessons in order to better handle whatever life may throw at them.

Here are some of the stories told in ancient and modern-day Yorubaland.

Akiti the Hunter

Akiti was a hunter known to have conquered man and animal alike. No animal crossed his path and went scot-free, be it snakes, lions, wolves, or leopards. Because of this, he called himself the "King of the Forest."

His triumph over animals made him prideful, and everyone feared him. He had forgotten that there was one animal that he had not yet encountered—the elephant.

The elephant was angry that Akiti was calling himself king because the elephant was already known to be the King of the Forest. So, the elephant challenged Akiti to a battle. Akiti threw a sharp spear at the elephant, but the elephant's hide protected it. Then Akiti used his knife, bow, and poisoned arrows, but his efforts were worthless.

Seeing that the elephant had a charm that protected it from weapons, Akiti used his charm to turn into a lion and lunged toward the elephant. The elephant simply threw him off.

Next, he changed into a snake, but he was unsuccessful in crushing the elephant to death. Finally, he transformed into a fly and flew into the elephant's ear, deep into the elephant's heart. Then he drove his hunting knife through its heart. The elephant didn't survive this one.

At last, no one questioned Akiti's name. He was truly the King of the Forest.

The Iroko Tree

There was a time when the Yorubas avoided the big tree in the forest. The tree referred to as "Iroko" was avoided because an old man inhabited it. At night, the old man walked around, shining his torch and instilling fear in travelers. Anyone that saw the old Iroko-man ran away from him as if they were mad and died soon after.

The thickness of the Iroko made the tree appealing to woodcutters, but they encountered misfortune when cutting it down, as their attempts caused them and their families to experience bad omens every day.

Every piece of furniture produced with Iroko-wood always groans and creaks at night. These noises are due to the old man trying to escape so that he can wander about again.

Why Women Have Long Hair

Once upon a time, two women quarreled, and one of them decided to make the other suffer. She dug a hole in the middle of the road leading from the other woman's house to the village well. The next morning, the other woman followed her friends to fetch water. While they were traveling, she fell into the pit. She screamed for help, and her friends came to rescue her. They managed to grip her by the hair and draw her up. But the more they pulled at her hair, the more her hair stretched.

They succeeded in pulling her out, but she was ashamed of how her hair was as long as her arm, so she ran away to hide. Later on, she noticed that her long hair was beautiful, and she swelled with pride. She began to shun the women with short hair. This made the short-haired women jealous and ashamed of themselves.

So, each of them jumped into the pit while their friends pulled them out by their hair. This stretched their hair as well. After this, every woman was born with long hair.

The Leopard Man

A beautiful stranger strolled about a village and never uttered a word. The maidens in the village were in love with him and wished to be his bride. Soon after, he disappeared into the forest.

One month later, he came in sight again, and one of the maidens who was in love with him followed him into the forest. He noticed her following him, and he turned around and begged her to go back. She refused and said, "I will never leave you, and wherever you go, I will follow."

"Beautiful maiden, you will regret it," he said as he trotted on. Both of them went deep into the forest and stopped at a tree with a leopard skin laid at its foot. He explained to her that he was allowed to go about the village once a month as a man but that he was actually a leopard. He told her that once he changed into his natural form, he would tear her into pieces.

Once he put the skin on, he immediately changed into a leopard and chased after her. The maiden was very fast, probably due to adrenaline, so it was difficult for him to catch her. As he chased her, he sang that he would tear her into pieces while she sang that he would never catch her.

A while later, she came across a river, and it seemed as if he would catch her after all. However, a tree by the corner of the river pitied her and bent over so she could cross the river. Finally, she reached the end of the forest and entered the village. The leopard was sad that he couldn't catch his prey and disappeared into the forest, never to be seen again.

The Three Deaths of Tortoise

Many animals hated Tortoise, and they planned to kill him. While he was asleep one night, they set his hut on fire. As the flames roared, they were convinced that he could not escape and said to themselves, "He cannot escape. He will die."

Tortoise had coiled himself into his shell and wasn't scarred by the fire. The next morning, they were surprised to see him walking the streets of the village. Then they gathered for another plan, and this time, they flung Tortoise into a pool of water. They said to themselves, "The pool is deep. He will drown."

Tortoise pulled himself into his shell and didn't drown. At noon, the sun shone strongly and dried the pool. His enemies were again surprised to see him again walking the streets of the village as though nothing had happened.

They had already come up with another plan by the next day. This time, they were certain that he would not escape. They dug a deep pit in the ground and buried Tortoise. They put a bamboo stake in the spot to mark the place.

A man passing by saw the bamboo stake and thought someone had buried treasure there. So, he called his friends to help him dig. They dug and dug and found Tortoise asleep in his shell. Tortoise walked about the village with excitement, once more surprising his enemies.

They finally gave up, saying to themselves, "He has a charm, and we shall never be able to kill him."

How The Leopard Got His Spots (Version 1)

The leopard didn't always have spots; once upon a time, his skin color was like that of a lion. But one day, Akiti the Hunter chased after him, and he was afraid that Akiti would kill him. So, he ate the root of a magic plant so that he would remain unaffected by Akiti's weapons.

Not long after, Akiti saw him among the trees and shot poisoned arrows at him, but the leopard escaped. These poisoned arrows created black spots on his body, allowing him to blend amongst the trees with the help of the sun and the shadows.

This makes it difficult for hunters to catch him even today.

How The Leopard Got His Spots (Version 2)

Before, the leopard had very dark skin. He was strolling one day in a compound when he noticed a woman bathing in a hut. The leopard circled the hut, waiting for his prey to step out. But he was very hungry and couldn't wait anymore. He went into the hut, shocking the woman to her bones. She screamed in fear and threw her loofah filled with soap at him.

He fled, covered with soap from head to foot, which he still has on to this very day.

Isokun and the Baby

Dekun, a king, had a wife called Isokun. She bore him no children, which created sadness and tension in the palace. One day, Isokun went missing. Everyone searched for her, but no one could find her. They didn't know that she had gone to plead with the gods of the land for a child. She went far and wide, but none of the gods had pity on her.

She headed back to her village, devastated by the gods' refusal. On her way, she saw an old woman asleep by the road with her two-day-old baby. Isokun stole the baby and hurried to the palace. She explained to the king that she went to the gods to give her a child and that her prayers were answered. The palace rejoiced. Sacrifices were made, and a great feast ensued.

The real mother finally woke up and saw that her baby was gone. Her efforts to find her baby were futile, but she was not ready to give up. She continued her search until she got to the palace. It was easy for her to enter because of the feast that was taking place.

The baby had been crying because of hunger, and Isokun could not feed him. She was unsuccessful in trying to pacify him without being suspicious. The old woman, drawn by the baby's noise, snatched the baby from Isokun and breastfed him, which comforted him immediately.

A few moments later, everyone knew that Isokun had lied. The old woman left with her baby, and Isokun fled the palace because she feared the king's anger. She never returned.

The Ants and the Treasure

There was a very poor man that cared for animals. Even though he had very little, he always left grains of corn and beans for his parrot. To pacify the ants from attacking his few possessions, he always spread tidbits of these grains on the floor, hoping it would be enough for them.

The ants were grateful for his actions.

In the same village, there was a rich man who refused to spend his money. He had stolen someone's gold and kept it in the corner of his hut. He watched over it day and night. Every living thing that crossed his path he killed and crushed, even the birds and the ants. He hated everything except his gold.

This angered the ants because he had killed a substantial number of their kind, so they decided to punish him. After discussing it, they came up with an idea. They wanted to take the gold to the poor man's house. So, they dug a tunnel, with one end at the poor man's house and the other at the rich man's house.

The very night that they completed the tunnel, a large swarm of ants carried a part of the gold through the tunnel to the poor man's house. The following day, the poor man was very excited that the gods had sent the gold. He kept the gold in a corner and covered it with a cloth.

Meanwhile, the rich man had discovered that a huge part of the gold was gone. He was confused as to how it had happened because he kept watch all night. The next night, the ants carried another part of the gold down the tunnel. Again, the poor man was happy, while the rich man was furious.

The third night, the ants successfully moved all of the gold from the rich man's home to the poor man's house. The rich man was devastated and called his neighbors. He explained how his gold had disappeared in three days. He emphasized that no one had entered his hut and that he was certain that it was stolen through witchcraft.

They helped him search his house and discovered the tunnel. Obviously, someone had stolen it through the tunnel, so they went through the tunnel to discover its other end. They found the poor man's house and discovered the gold.

The poor man protested that he couldn't have stolen it through a small tunnel. The rich man's neighbors accused him of using witchcraft to make himself small and stealing the gold at night. They punished him by shutting him in his hut. The next day, they decided to burn him alive.

When the ants saw what had happened, they were baffled and thought of how to help their friend from being executed. There was no other option than for them to eat the hut. This they did in a few hours, and the poor man was dazed to find himself in an open space. But he didn't think twice. He escaped into the forest, never to return again.

The next morning, the villagers came and saw that the ants had been responsible for releasing the man. They thought the gods had taken the punishment into their own hands by sending the ants to eat both the hut and the poor man.

Until today, only the ants know that's not the truth.

The Head

In a certain village, the villagers coexisted without bodies. They had only heads. They moved about by jumping, so they never went far.

One of the heads wished to see the world, so he left the village one morning in secret. He met a woman who was looking out the window and asked if she could lend him a torso. The woman agreed. She lent him the torso of her slave, and the head thanked her and went on his way.

Later, he met a man sleeping under the tree and asked if he could lend him his arms since the man wasn't using them. The man agreed and lent him his arms. The head thanked him and went on his way.

Later on, he stopped at a river where some fishermen were singing and fishing. He asked if one of them could lend him a pair of legs as they were sitting and not using their legs at that moment. One of the men agreed and lent the adventurous man his legs. He thanked the man and went on his way.

Now, his body was complete. He had a torso, arms, legs, and a head.

He headed to a village, where onlookers tossed coins to maidens as the maidens danced. He tossed all his coins to a maiden, and she admired his handsomeness. She asked him to marry her and take her to his village.

He married the lady, and they set out the next day. When they reached the riverbank, he pulled off the legs and gave them to the fisherman. Later, they reached the tree where that man was still sleeping, and the head gave his arms back to him. Finally, they reached the cottage where he met the woman and gave her the torso.

When the maiden saw that he was just a head, she was terrified and ran as fast as she could. Since the head had no arms, legs, or body, he couldn't catch her, so he lost her forever.

Erin and Erinomi (The Land and the Water Elephants)

The tortoise was known to cause trouble amongst the animals. One day, while walking alongside the river, the tortoise met the elephant and told him, "The hippo brags that you are weak and cannot even muster the strength to haul a log of wood from the water."

"That is not true!" the elephant cried. To prove how strong he was, the elephant told the tortoise to bind a piece of twine to his trunk and fix the other end to a tree. The tortoise did as he was told, then went down to the river and pulled the same prank on the hippo. The tortoise started by saying that, "The elephant is boastful of his strength and proclaims you a weakling that cannot fell a tree."

Surprised, the hippo cried, "That is not true! I can bring down any tree." Then the tortoise told him that he had fastened twine to a tree and that he could bind the other end to the hippo. The hippo agreed to tie the twine to his tusk.

The animals pulled and pulled, one at each end, but neither gave way. After a while, the hippo decided to rest. And the elephant decided to go to the river to drink some water. There, they found that the tortoise had deceived them. Angrily, they searched all over for the tortoise, but he was already long gone.

Conclusion

After Nigeria was liberated in 1960, the surviving ancient Yoruba kingdoms maintained their monarchs, but today, many of the rulers do not have the power their ancestors used to wield. However, they are all respected by their subjects and are given honorary reverence by the government of Nigeria.

The kingdoms are not as big as they used to be because they have been divided into administrative boundaries (states) by the ruling government of Nigeria. The first division of Nigeria was done in 1967 by the military head of state, General Yakubu Gowon.

As mentioned in the book, Yorubas are all over the world. This is partially due to the slave trade but primarily due to the large rate of emigration of Africans from third-world countries to developed countries. The Yorubas got into the slave trade later than most, which resulted in many Yorubas still having knowledge of their culture and language when slavery was abolished. This allowed them to establish diaspora communities more easily after they were freed. Within these diaspora communities, they have kept their culture and are known for their different traditional attires and parties, which are known as *owambes.*

There is at least one Yoruba person in almost every country, and coupled with their love for promoting their culture and their language, the Yorubas are very popular. They are also known to be disciplined, hardworking, and industrious.

This comprehensive book draws on rare historical books, documentaries, and revelations from people to cover the origin of the Yoruba people and their ancestral heroes, traditions, economy, and politics.

It is important to note that the stories, events, and figures in this book are just a glimpse of who the Yoruba people actually are. There are still many aspects of their history that are yet to be told. However, we hope this book achieved its aim of providing a captivating introductory guide through the history of the Yoruba people.

Part 2: History of West Africa

A Captivating Guide to West African History, Starting from Ancient Civilizations through the Medieval Period to the Present

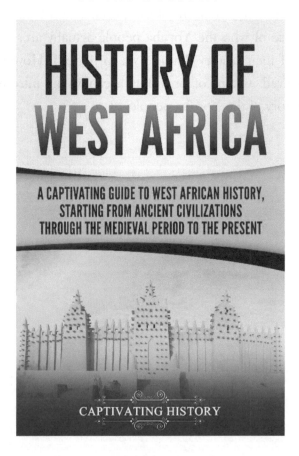

Introduction

West Africa is one of the most fascinating areas in the world. It consists of sixteen independent countries and is home to close to 381 million people. The area is also the fastest-growing economic region in Africa. Present-day West Africa boasts beautiful architecture, appealing cultures, and a diverse population of people. While many of the countries that make up the region only gained their independence from European countries a few decades ago, they are creating their own identities in the global economy and are drawing thousands of tourists, historians among them.

What makes West Africa so compelling to renowned historians, archaeologists, and amateur history enthusiasts? The region has an extremely interesting history that features several prominent empires as well as some of the most underrated but influential leaders in history. Learn about the mighty Mali Empire and the effects of traditional African religions, along with Islam and Christianity, on the local history and cultures in different parts of the region. Find out more about interesting figures such as Mansa Musa and Sundiata Keita, among many others. This book also contains incredible stories of the rise and fall of several dynasties and the power struggles in between.

We will start off with a brief explanation of what makes West Africa so unique in terms of ecology and geographic location. The first section of the book is dedicated to exploring the prehistory of this captivating area and details how the early West Africans developed their civilizations into mighty kingdoms that organized trade and took care of massive territories.

In time, these kingdoms were conquered by burgeoning empires that took advantage of lucrative trade routes from the north to the south of Africa. The second section of this book will discuss the most powerful empires in West African history and provides a glimpse into the lives of ordinary and wealthy citizens alike. These empires were the Mali, Ghana, and Songhai Empires, which all left a lasting impression on world history. These empires and other influential kingdoms ruled from mankind's early history well into medieval times. They brought great wealth to the people and were ruled by impressive warriors and politicians.

However, these empires were unable to fight off the threat of invading Europeans. The third section of this book will discuss the period of European colonialism, slavery, and the effects of these on modern West African countries. For hundreds of years, the area was dominated by foreign powers that exploited the population and the region's rich natural resources, which left a lasting impact on everything from the economy to local cultures. Despite these hardships, West Africa is a vibrant and incredible part of Africa with a bright future.

Follow the rise, fall, and development of a massive part of the African continent in this easy-to-read book. Discover a melting pot of African, Arabic, and European history hidden in the tropical forests and deserts of West Africa that will transform your knowledge of mankind's collective history.

Section 1:
Ancient African Civilizations

Chapter 1 – What is West Africa?

West Africa is a sub-region of the African continent that is made up of sixteen different countries. Those countries are Benin, Burkina Faso, Cape Verde, Côte D'Ivoire, Gambia (also known as The Gambia), Ghana, Guinea, Guinea-Bissau, Liberia, Mali, Mauritania, Niger, Nigeria, Senegal, Sierra Leone, and Togo. This vast region of land is home to many different cultures, religions, and environments. Ranging from arid deserts to sandy beaches to tropical jungles, West Africa boasts a diverse range of terrain that was at one time the home of several different kingdoms.

This diverse environment meant that the West Africans had different resources at their disposal and were part of some of the most lucrative trade routes in history. A quick look into what makes West Africa so unique will form the foundation of understanding the area's varied and dynamic history.

Ancient West African Ecology and Geography

West Africa takes up about one-fifth of the African continent. Most of that land is about three hundred meters above sea level, which means that most of West Africa is made up out of low-lying plains. The northern part of the region is made up of desert-like land that borders the Sahara. Rainfall is scarce. Meanwhile, the southern part is made up of forests where rain is more common. Vegetation ranges from arid plains to tall trees and massive forests. Many of these forests grow close to the Atlantic coast.

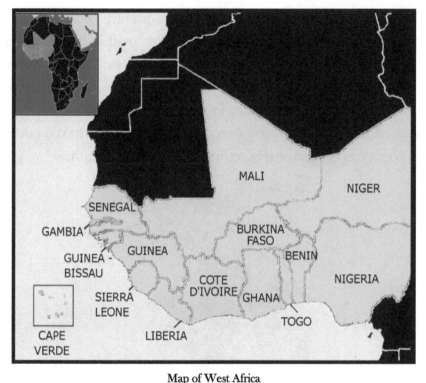

Map of West Africa
https://commons.wikimedia.org/wiki/File:Map_of_West_AFrica.gif

Despite belonging to the same region on a map, West Africa features incredibly diverse physical environments. These environments are completely contradictory, as there are savannahs, forests, lowlands, and highlands. The people of the region had to quickly adapt to their environments, which led to the development of contrasting cultures and farming practices. This is important to note because farming was (and still is) an integral part of West African life.

In the forested areas, the development of permanent crops, such as palm oil, kola nuts, and coffee and cocoa beans, was very important because the land couldn't sustain periodic crops for large amounts of time. In the savannahs, the farms are larger, but there are fewer people who choose to live there since rainfall isn't assured, which means crops can easily fail.

The discovery of cocoa beans would have massive consequences for the West African region. Cocoa beans were first used in South America, and European explorers brought the plant back to Europe, where it became a desirable commodity. In time, the Portuguese planted cocoa trees on an island close to Gabon in the early 1800s. By the late 1800s, millions of kilograms of cocoa were being exported from West Africa. Soon, cocoa was being grown in several West African countries.

Cocoa Tree
https://commons.wikimedia.org/wiki/File:Fotg_cocoa_d091_cacao_tree_and_seedling.png

Besides cocoa, West Africa is also home to numerous other important plants, including the kola nut. This nut is grown all over the world, but it originated in West Africa, where it was extremely popular thanks to the caffeine it contains. Many cultures use the kola nut in sacred and social rituals, and it is also known to have medicinal properties. West African captives took the nuts along with them when they were transported by slave ships, which took the kola nut all over the world.

Kola nut

There are many important inland bodies of water, which were used for trade and became the home of many different civilizations. The most notable ones are Lake Chad, the Niger River system, and the Senegal River, among others. These rivers all have complex systems that ensure the surrounding lands are well watered and fertile.

For most of its history, West Africa was home to many different species of animals, including lions, elephants, leopards, and hippopotami. Unfortunately, when the land was colonized, many British and French settlers seized the opportunity to export exotic hunting trophies, meat, skins, and products, such as ivory. This led to extensive hunting that decimated the animal population. By the 20th century, most of the exotic animals in the area were dead. Unfortunately, by the early 1900s, the elephant population in Gambia was completely extinct. The British tried to curb hunting, but by then, it was too late. Today, the last exotic animals are confined to nature reservations and sanctuaries.

Many of the environments in West Africa are known for being harsh due to uncertain weather patterns, which makes life difficult, but the people of the region came up with unique ways to survive. For thousands of years, the people of West Africa made the most of their environment. And thanks to the diversity in the landscape, the people had plenty of unique items that could be traded. This led to the development of extensive trade routes that led from North to South Africa. Thanks to its advantageous position along these routes, West Africa profited massively from trade, and in time, powerful empires grew in some of the harshest environments in the world.

Trade Routes

Trade played a crucial role in the West African economy, and it helped build some of the most important kingdoms in the area. There were trade routes that ran all over Africa and transported a myriad of goods to places as far away as India and Europe. Items such as the kola nut, metal, cloth, beads, slaves, and ivory were highly sought after and brought great wealth to traders. While these items certainly boosted economies, the most important items were gold and salt, both of which were extremely valuable commodities.

In time, major cities began to spring up along these bustling trade routes. Impressive cities such as Timbuktu, Gao, Agadez, Djenné, and Sijilmasa became important destinations on ancient maps and were almost always filled to the brim with traders and valuable goods. Traders needed to deal with harsh environments and traveled in caravans for safety. The caravans needed to cross the arid Sahara region to get to their destinations, as the sub-Saharan area was rich in resources.

Crossing the Sahara presented unique challenges, but the domestication of camels allowed traders to travel farther and more efficiently. The Berber people were among the first to use camels, and their caravans crossed the Sahara as early as the 1ˢᵗ millennium CE. For hundreds of years, they were the link between North and West Africa. The trans-Saharan trade routes flourished, as massive caravans, sometimes comprised of as many as ten thousand camels, carried gold and salt from all parts of Africa to the rest of the world. Since the demand for gold surged in Mediterranean kingdoms, which needed the precious metal for coins and luxury items, the trans-Saharan trade routes flourished.

Arab merchants set up shop in Morocco and traded with the Berber people, who were adept at traversing the Sahara. This extensive trade may have helped several kingdoms come into power. West Africa had more than enough gold, and the local people were expert miners and craftsmen, but for a long period of time, they were unwilling to share the source of their gold with traders. The Soninke people, in particular, were determined to keep their mines a secret from the outside world.

In time, Ghana was able to take control of an important trade route, allowing it to become a mighty empire. However, the empire eventually fell, and Mali emerged as a stronger power. Despite the lucrative trade that took place, gold wasn't exported in massive quantities. Instead, a relatively small amount was taken from Africa, but the wealth of West Africa's empires was known all throughout the world. In a time when most countries were struggling to find gold to make their coins, the city of Timbuktu used golden coins that didn't bear any stamps.

While gold was in demand, salt was almost just as valuable. The Sahara contained natural salt deposits, which were taken from the desert to busy trading centers where it was traded for gold dust. There weren't many salt deposits in West Africa, which made it a highly sought-after commodity. Salt was needed to dry meat and was especially necessary in the dry areas where fresh produce was hard to come by. The mineral was mined in parts of the desert and transported via camel to where it needed to go. Unfortunately, salt rocks were difficult to carry, which made transporting the mineral expensive. It also wasn't mined fast enough to satisfy the demand, and these two factors were enough to push the price of salt upward until it matched the price of gold.

Salt was an essential part of life for many people, which made it one of the most profitable minerals in the world. Gold and salt were extremely valuable and brought great wealth to whoever controlled the trade routes, which meant that fights for control of the routes sometimes determined the fate of entire empires.

Islamic Influence

Before the spread of Islam, the people of West Africa had their own traditional religions, which differed according to where people lived or what culture they belonged to. A unified faith allowed rulers to control larger territories and strengthen their authority. History proves that a united empire is easier to control, and Islam gave people a sense of belonging that united them as a larger community. Along with a new religion, Islam also gave people a common justice system that made ruling a lot easier.

In the 7th century CE, North Africa was conquered by the Arabs, who brought their religion with them. By then, the trans-Saharan trade was in full swing, which made it easier for missionaries and scholars to travel and take their religion with them. Unlike many other religions, these Muslim travelers didn't force people to convert, so the change from smaller traditional religions to Islam was largely peaceful. Local rulers either converted to the religion or allowed their Muslim communities to live in peace.

The Umayyad Caliphate of Damascus conquered North Africa with its military and quickly established rule there. Trade continued, and the Berbers were converted to Islam, which made it easier for the religion to spread since they had contact with most civilizations in Africa. The religion was often adopted by African rulers, as they saw the benefit of a unified kingdom or recognized that conversion would be beneficial for trading. Islam provided a system that relied on a moral code, as well as a common set of laws and codes that helped to enhance an already lucrative trading system.

In time, Arab traders arrived in East Africa from the Red Sea, and soon Islam swept through most of Africa. Over time, there were several violent conflicts between Christian kingdoms, Muslim societies, and communities where the ancient African traditional religions persisted. However, the Islamic influence was more than just spiritual. It also affected things such as architecture, art, administration, and language. While many people peacefully converted to Islam, that doesn't mean that the religion remained pure, as many cultures simply added their traditional practices to their new faith, which led to a hybrid religion that incorporated aspects of Islam and traditional African religions. Wherever Arab travelers went, they took their religion with them, and over six centuries, the religion had spread over most of the continent.

However, not all the African kingdoms were enthusiastic about the spread of Islam. In Ghana, the kings simply tolerated the Muslim traders and allowed people to convert if they wished to do so. This resulted in a blended culture. The city of Koumbi Saleh, which was the capital of Ghana, was split into two, with the Muslims on one side and followers of indigenous religions on the other. This meant that one side of the city featured mosques while the other was full of shrines. For a long time, the two cultures simply existed side by side.

In other kingdoms, Islam was embraced enthusiastically. For example, Mansa Musa I, the king of Mali, visited Arab cities and brought back scholars and architects who, in turn, brought their ideas and practices with them. Schools and mosques were built, and major cities, such as Timbuktu, became predominantly Muslim, which was reflected in every aspect of ordinary life. Soon, Islam became an African religion, and it became closely intertwined with the local cultures and traditions.

While Islam spread peacefully throughout most of the continent, this spread was resisted by African kingdoms in the south, which led to violent conflicts. The violence only increased when Portuguese explorers landed in West and East Africa, bringing their staunch Christian beliefs with them.

European Influence

In the 15th century, Portuguese sailors landed on the coast of Guinea and brought about a new age in West African history. Portugal was not a wealthy country, but through maritime trade, the Portuguese were able to enrich and strengthen their kingdom. Their main goal at this time was to set up trade with both Asia and Africa, and even though they found a wealth of resources in Africa, their main goal was to trade with India and the East Indies. The Portuguese wanted complete control of trade with West Africa and took decisive steps to exclude others from trading with the region.

They found that the people of Ghana were willing to trade gold with them in exchange for cloth and other metals. In Europe, this coastline became known as the Gold Coast. The Portuguese were only interested in trade at that time and built a fort called São Jorge da Mina to protect those interests. Soon, other forts were built. However, since Portugal wasn't able to produce the resources that were desirable in their own land, they had to expand their trade to reach other African countries. During this time, European influence was minimal, as Portugal did a good job of protecting the Gold Coast from other European countries. The Portuguese introduced Christianity to the West Africans, and some elements of the Portuguese language were adopted, but other than that, their impact was relatively minimal.

Fort São Jorge da Mina today
Francisco Anzola, CC BY 2.0 <https://creativecommons.org/licenses/by/2.0>, via Wikimedia Commons https://commons.wikimedia.org/wiki/File:Elmina_Castle_and_Fort_(3587087813).jpg

Portuguese explorers took items such as gold, ivory, and art back to their homes. While Europeans painted Africa as a savage and backward continent, nothing could have been further from the truth. The continent hosted vibrant and profitable trade routes and interacted freely with North Africa and the Middle East. One of the world's oldest universities was located in Timbuktu, and scholars lived in most African cities. African artworks show how connected the different cultures were and how many areas developed traditional pieces that were distinctive to their area. Unfortunately, the Europeans had discovered the value of the continent, and many different European countries began staking claims on various parts of Africa. Around the 16th century, the transatlantic slave trade developed, and over the next few centuries, millions of Africans were stolen from their homes and transported throughout the world.

Entire villages and ethnic groups were simply taken, while those remaining turned on each other in an effort to avoid being sold themselves. While the slave trade had always been a part of the world economy, the transatlantic slave trade took staggering numbers of people away from their homes, which decimated kingdoms and cultures. Once the slave trade started dying down, Africa was far from safe. Between 1884 and 1885, the Berlin Conference was hosted without any Africans in attendance. The European powers drew borders on the African maps and took whatever they wanted. These new borders were imposed without any care about geographical or ethnic factors. The indifferent European rulers split tribes and families apart, and the effects of the Berlin Conference are still felt in modern-day Africa.

In time, African leaders began declaring their independence and reclaiming their identities and heritages. One thing is for certain: West Africa has an intriguing history that began with prehistoric foragers who eventually became expert miners, tradesmen, and emperors.

Before the influence of Islam and Europeans, West Africa was the home of several vibrant and advanced cultures that predated the massive empires that rose in medieval times and featured traces of outside influences.

Chapter 2 – Dhar Tichitt and Djenné-Djenno: Home of the Ancients

As with most regions, the early people of West Africa were nomadic hunter-gatherers who did the best they could in a harsh and changeable world. Over time, they settled down and became farmers and eventually built great civilizations. Since West Africa has a number of different environments, the ancient people who lived there traveled as much as possible to take advantage of favorable environments.

As people began working with tools and learning to farm the land they previously traveled, some people settled in places like Dhar Tichitt and Dhar Walata. These settlements are remarkably well preserved and provide historians with a rare and valuable glimpse into the lives of the people who made a home there. As urbanization began to take hold of Africa, places like Djenné-Djenno became centers of urban living.

The journey from nomads to established cities is always interesting, and West Africa is no different.

Prehistoric West Africa

Uncovering the secrets of West Africa's prehistory has proved to be a challenging task for historians. Unlike other parts of Africa, which offer many clues about their prehistory in the form of the Bantu expansion or Swahili trading posts, West Africa offers up no such clues. However, that doesn't mean that there's nothing to find. West Africa is a massive stretch of land, and historians have only scratched the surface of discovering what treasures lay hidden beneath the surface. Historians have been able to observe several interesting factors that give them an idea of West Africa's prehistory.

Prehistoric West African artifacts

Scientists have found evidence of drastic climate change in the Sahara. This indicates that people had to travel to different areas out of necessity. Interestingly, there are still nomadic people who live in the Sahara, and historians have theorized that the smaller nomadic tribes were once part of larger groups of people who didn't need to travel as much. Evidence shows that tool-using people were living in West Africa as early as the Middle Pleistocene era. As the weather in the region changed, people began to migrate to different areas.

People began creating pottery and weapons around 9400 BCE. For much of West Africa's early history, the Sahara was a well-watered area that supported life and could be used to maintain flocks of animals. Historians have found evidence that Barbary sheep were farmed in the Sahara. Unfortunately, the climate began to change, and the people likely followed the water, leaving behind some people who adapted to a nomadic way of life and found ways to thrive in the harsh desert.

The people who left the Sahara were met by hunter-gatherers who existed in other parts of West Africa. Soon, the people mingled and became part of larger groups. As people began herding cattle and growing crops, an intricate social structure began to develop, as people took on different roles within society. Cattle was a valuable resource that was traded and formed the basis of the emerging social structure. Thankfully, there are still ancient settlements that exist today and are well preserved.

As a social hierarchy developed around 4000 BCE, historians have found evidence that the Mandé people created the Tichitt culture. The Mandé people can be found all over West Africa. They created an intricate culture that can be studied due to the artifacts that were left behind. The Tichitt culture formed the basis for advanced civilizations that can be found at ancient West African settlements, such as Dhar Tichitt.

The Mandé people are thought to have developed farming practices in West Africa. The various languages that developed from the Mandé people formed the basis of the primary language family in parts of West Africa. Eventually, the Mandé split into groups, with the East Mandé and

West Mandé being the most influential. The East Mandé went on to form the Soninke culture that became the foundation of the Ghana Empire, while the West Mandé became the Malinke who formed the Mali Empire.

Dhar Tichitt

Not much is known about the Tichitt culture, which is a shame since it formed one of the oldest civilizations in West Africa. Before the Tichitt culture, people traveled in small groups, and the earliest settlements that have been found were very basic and wouldn't have been used for long periods of time. All of that changed as the Tichitt culture developed and complex settlements were built.

Dhar Tichitt was built on a sandstone cliff that is part of a series in the south of Mauritania and south of the Sahara. Several settlements were built along the cliffs. People there concentrated on herding animals, especially cattle, which eventually became a status symbol, and growing crops. Thanks to abundant water sources, life was able to flourish in the region, which probably made it easier for people to make their homes there.

Although people lived in Dhar Tichitt all throughout the year, there seem to be some areas where people lived when the dry season came and others where they lived during the rainy seasons. When the region was dry, people would move to the lowlands and live in temporary camps close to sources of water. However, when the rains came, the people would move to higher ground, where they built structures out of stone. The people who lived in Dhar Tichitt built homes, granaries, and enclosures for their livestock. In some areas, historians have found evidence of street-like layouts, which gives an idea of how advanced this early society was.

Life in Dhar Tichitt

The people at Dhar Tichitt herded cattle, sheep, and goats, but they also lived alongside wild animals, such as gazelle, crocodiles, and hippopotami. They also practiced animal husbandry and learned how to grow specific crops. The Tichitt people cultivated millet but otherwise mostly relied on gathering wild crops. There would have been plenty to eat, and adapting to the changing seasons meant that the people of the area could get the full benefit of the land. It was a clever way to adapt to an often harsh and changeable environment.

Millet grain
Couleur https://pixabay.com/users/couleur-1195798/, CC BY-SA 4.0
<https://creativecommons.org/licenses/by-sa/4.0>, via Wikimedia Commons
https://commons.wikimedia.org/wiki/File:Millet-1697117_1920.jpg

The settlers who occupied the site used tools to build their structures and learned to build stone walls that would protect their boundaries and gardens. They also proved to be craftsmen who created weapons for hunting and pieces of pottery. As time went on, they began developing an intricate culture, and some elements of that ancient culture can be found in later cities, such as Koumbi Saleh.

As the culture developed, so did the social hierarchy. More people began to inhabit the area, which meant that the land needed to be used more carefully, especially since the desert was slowly creeping closer. The longer the Tichitt people lived in the area, the more advanced their tools became. Granaries, millstones, and ceramics in the area have been excavated and show that the Tichitt people had become adept at working with millet. In time, the people even began decorating their ceramics and pottery in a distinctive style.

Life in the area would have revolved around working in the gardens, hunting for meat, and preserving food. As the people began using tools and weapons, they would have found the need to sharpen axes and maintain their tools. The same stones that were used to sharpen their axes were also used to sand down quartzite and similar stones to make beads, bracelets, and rings.

Neighboring Settlements

The cliff series that hosted Dhar Tichitt was also the home of the ancient settlements of Dhar Walata, Dhar Néma, and Dhar Tagant. The settlements provide a lot of insight about one of the earliest sedentary communities in Africa, and historians are still excavating and studying the sites. While conducting their research, archaeologists found that a close link existed between the ancient settlements and have found evidence of the Tichitt culture among the ruins of all the settlements.

Historians have identified a few main components of the Tichitt culture, namely the herding of cattle, the cultivation of millet, the use of simple-styled ceramics, and distinctive granaries. Prior to 4000 BCE, the area housed several lakes that would have created an oasis, which would have made it easier to build settlements.

As at Dhar Tichitt, the people in the neighboring settlements adopted an agropastoral way of life, and in time, they began building granaries and used tools. As time went on, the people began to use iron for their tools and weapons. This is evidenced by the discovery of several iron-smelting sites in the area. As the Tichitt culture developed, more people began to live in the settlements, which presented the need for a social hierarchy.

Historians have found that the Tichitt people were also accomplished at making beads and jewelry out of different types of stone in the area, including quartzite. They would take the metamorphic rock and polish it until it could be used for decoration. These objects were highly prized, and historians have found individuals who were buried with their jewelry.

The Tichitt people also left behind rock art, which allows historians to gain a glimpse of the mysterious ancient culture. The people painted hunting scenes and left behind pictures on funerary monuments. The art has survived for thousands of years and tells the story of this ancient culture and how its people interacted with their environment.

Rock art at Dhar Tichitt

While Dhar Tichitt and its surroundings served as a good home for many centuries, it eventually faded and all but disappeared. The decline of the Tichitt culture is shrouded in mystery, although there are a few different theories. The prevailing theory is that the encroaching desert forced the people to leave the settlements behind, while the arrival of the Berber people in the 1ˢᵗ millennium led to violent conflicts. The Berbers had superior weapons and rock art in the area, which shows that the Berbers won many of the conflicts. These factors could mean that the Berbers eventually replaced the Tichitt culture or that the two cultures eventually merged.

Djenné-Djenno

While Dhar Tichitt was an impressive settlement for its time, it was eventually abandoned, and people began to live in larger settlements that gradually became cities. One of the oldest cities in West Africa is Djenné-Djenno (or Old Jenne), which is located in the country of Mali and was established around 250 BCE. The city was located in a fertile area and positioned along one of the sub-Saharan trade routes. These factors ensured that the city flourished and existed for hundreds of years. The city is now the home of several archaeological sites named Kaniana, Tonomba, and Hambarkétolo.

The people of the city had access to the Niger River and its connected waterways, which meant that they could catch different types of fish to feed themselves and sell to others. The city was also located on a floodplain, which made it easier to grow crops such as rice, vegetables, fruit, and grain. The abundance of food meant that when trade routes developed, the inhabitants of the city had plenty of resources to trade.

8. Aerial view of the Niger River

Traders would take food, such as grain, fish oil, and dried fish, toward the north to the savannahs of modern-day Sudan and to the south of Africa. The people of the city became efficient traders, and they would exchange their resources for stones, iron ore, copper, gold, beads, and salt. Eventually, the inhabitants of the city developed distinctive pottery that they also exported.

They also figured out how to work with iron and copper, which led to better weapons and tools, as well as a prosperous metalworking industry.

Life in Djenné-Djenno

The inhabitants of the city enjoyed a more sophisticated lifestyle than their neighbors, who lived in smaller settlements. During this time, the Saharan trade routes were becoming more intricate and essential to the economies of the surrounding areas. Trade would have been a massive part of the city's economy, and many traders would have lived in the city.

Ordinary people would have spent their time fishing and cultivating crops. Most of the houses in the area were made of mudbrick with stone foundations. The people built their homes on small hills to avoid being swept away during the rainy season. The city was also home to artisans, who created distinctive sculptures and pieces of pottery that would have been sold to traders or used to decorate local homes.

Historians have found remains of the pre-Islamic culture that inhabited the city. The people of that era left behind pottery, grinders, funerary jars, and even buildings that were free from the influences of the religion that would eventually sweep through the region. Unfortunately, much of the early culture of Djenné-Djenno remains unknown since the people didn't develop a writing system.

The absence of writing means that it's nearly impossible to know how the early city was governed, but archaeologists have uncovered many clues that give insight into how the city functioned. It was a remarkably large settlement for its time, with a few smaller settlements that surrounded the main city. Historians have also found the presence of ancient workshops where artisans and metalworkers would have created pottery, sculptures, tools, and weapons.

Thanks to trade and the fertile land conditions, the elite of the city would have enjoyed a fairly luxurious lifestyle, and even the ordinary people would have enjoyed the city's prosperity. During its time, the city would have been one of the best destinations along the multiple trade routes that ran throughout the region. The city also boasted an impressive population of around 20,000 people during its peak and spanned about 300,000 square meters. Unfortunately, Djenné-Djenno was eventually abandoned and forgotten.

Djenné-Djenno's Decline

Eventually, the city fell into decline by the 9th century and was replaced with a completely new city named Djenné that was built a few miles away. It's not well known why the old city was abandoned, but by the 13th century, no one was living in the city anymore. Some of the city's history survived by means of oral traditions. According to this information, the population became too large for the settlement, and the people simply left. It's also possible that the new city, which was built by Muslim traders, was required because the old city was steeped in pagan religions that would have been reflected in the attitude of the people and the architecture.

Whatever the reason, Djenné-Djenno was an incredible city that flourished for hundreds of years and proved the profitability of trade with other parts of Africa. In time, the massive empires that would rise in West Africa would follow the example of the ancient city and use trade to build their wealth and power.

Djenné-Djenno's Legacy

For the past few decades, the site has been the focus of several archaeological excavations. Most of the buildings in the city were made from mudbricks and mud with stone foundations. This means that many of the walls have disappeared over time, which makes it difficult to know exactly what the buildings were used for. Historians haven't found any temple or palace sites but have found the foundation for a large wall that surrounded the city. The wall probably wasn't built to fortify the city but appears to have simply circled the city.

Many of the artifacts found in the city provide evidence of the bustling trade that once took place there. Historians have found gold jewelry and glass beads; the latter may have been brought all the way from India by way of camel caravans. They have also found intricate pottery that was probably used as decoration. The pieces were painted with vibrant colors and decorated with various patterns.

While no records exist of the early culture that lived in the city, historians have found interesting terracotta sculptures that may hint at what the people believed. These figurines often show a male riding a horse. Some of the figures are depicted as bowing or kneeling, and many of the sculptures were carefully carved and decorated with paint. Some of the figures feature carefully carved jewelry or weapons. Historians theorize that the figurines were used in ordinary homes and were probably used for shrines. It's possible that the ancient people of the city worshiped their ancestors and various spirits.

The terracotta sculptures of Djenné-Djenno sometimes raise more questions than answers since many of the figures seem to be suffering from illnesses or are depicted as being attacked by a snake. There are also several different types of burials that have been discovered in the city, which could mean that the people had different religions or belonged to different cultures.

Since the city remains shrouded in mystery due to a lack of written records, historians have a lot of work ahead of them as they uncover the secrets of Old Jenne. As the ancient city faded, other cultures became more powerful and wielded great influence throughout West Africa. Some of those cultures faded into history, but others maintained their influence over thousands of years. One such culture belongs to the Yoruba people, who built a holy city that withstood the test of time: the city of Ife.

Chapter 3 – Ile Ife: Birthplace of Mankind

Ile-Ife, or Ife, was established around 500 BCE and was the center of the Kingdom of Ife, which was established by the Yoruba people. The city is located in modern-day Nigeria and is still a religious center and the home of one of Nigeria's most prestigious universities, Obafemi Awolowo University. It is also part of Nigeria's Osun State. It was once the center of a prosperous kingdom, and it has survived many highs and lows during its history.

The Ooni of Ife's current palace

The_AyeniPaul, CC BY-SA 4.0 <https://creativecommons.org/licenses/by-sa/4.0>, via Wikimedia Commons https://commons.wikimedia.org/wiki/File:Palace_of_the_current_Ooni_of_Ife.jpg

The city was (and still is) an agricultural powerhouse, exporting products like grain, cacao, tobacco, cotton, and vegetables. It's known for being a holy city, and according to Yoruba tradition, it is the birthplace of mankind. Ife is an ancient city with a fascinating history, and the art that was produced there is legendary and breathtaking. It reached its peak in the Middle Ages, but the Kingdom of Ife suddenly disappeared in the 16th century. While there are many mysteries associated with the city, it still has a fascinating story to tell.

The Origin Myth

The Yoruba have their own theories about the origins of humans and are convinced that Ile-Ife is the birthplace of humankind. According to the myth, before the earth was created, there were only two elements—the sky above and the water below. The water was a chaotic state, while the gods lived in heaven. According to the myth, the supreme god, Olodumare, ordered his servant, Oduduwa, to create the earth. Oduduwa was an obedient servant who quickly began carrying out this monumental task.

He went down to earth with a calabash (a dried gourd that could be used as a container) full of sand. The calabash was attached to a chain, and Oduduwa took a five-toed fowl with him. Since the earth was filled with water, Oduduwa's first task was to create land. He did this by pouring the sand over the water and placing the fowl on the newly made land. As the fowl walked, the ground became solid. Soon, a chameleon was sent down to see if the fowl had done a good job. Some sections of water weren't touched by the sand and remained liquid. According to the myth, the chain that Oduduwa brought from heaven still remains in the city.

Calabash
Hyunjung Kim, CC0, via Wikimedia Commons
https://commons.wikimedia.org/wiki/File:Calabash_(Lagenaria_siceraria)_in_Seoul.jpg

In time, the god Obatala created humans out of clay, and Oduduwa became the first king of Ife. His children succeeded him and spread out to rule the other Yoruba states. While the myth has a neat conclusion, historians have found evidence that the Igbo people may have inhabited Ife before the Yoruba people. It is thought that King Oduduwa brought his army from the north and conquered the city, which later became the center of the Yoruba people's kingdom. Like many kings around the world and throughout time, King Oduduwa likely saw the benefit in associating himself with the divine. His descendants would have an easier time claiming absolute power if they descended from an actual god. Since not much is known about Ife's rulers, it is possible that this myth sprang up while King Oduduwa was still alive. This narrative also could have been crafted by his descendants. Either way, the myth gave the city a unique status among the other cities in the area and would have cemented its status as a sacred and holy city.

It's no surprise that Ife plays a major role in several Yoruba myths considering its religious status. The city's name means the "Place of Dispersion," and this is likely due to another myth concerning the ancient city. According to that myth, Oduduwa had sons and daughters who went on to rule their own states that formed part of the larger Yorubaland. This means that Oduduwa's lineage would have maintained complete control over the kingdom, and his family would have formed a mighty dynasty.

There is also evidence that the city went through periods where its settlement was interrupted. Much of the city's early history has been lost, and it's possible that when the occupation of the city was interrupted, the oral traditions weren't passed on to the later generations who went back to inhabit the city.

It is believed that sacrifices were made to gods and ancestors alike, and the king would have taken the lead in both the state and religion. Ife's religion combined elements of ancestor worship and animism. Religion likely played a massive part in the ordinary lives of Ife's residents since a lot of the art produced in the city seems to be linked to religion.

According to the Yoruba belief system, the energy that animated living things was present in everything. In a person, that energy was called *ase*, and a person's character, or *iwa*, would reflect that energy. A person's *ase* was always in their head, which may explain why a lot of ancient Ife art is focused on heads. This energy could be dangerous, especially if it belonged to a powerful person, which was why people in positions of power typically had veils over their mouths or faces. This was also depicted in ancient art. It also confirms the well-worn principle that mystery can also equal majesty, which would have lent credence to the rulers' divine right to rule. If people associated their leaders with their gods, they would follow those leaders unquestioningly.

Brass head from Ife

Due to the intricacy of ancient Ife art, it is possible that the art was used in religious rituals. Life in West Africa wasn't always easy, and even great cities faced enormous threats, both external and internal. However, Ife was regarded as a holy city and is still the home of the spiritual leader of the Yoruba people, the Ooni. Thanks to its status as the birthplace of mankind, the city of Ife was regarded as sacred and kept safe for hundreds of years.

Ife's Rise and Decline

Not much is known about the city's early days, but the founding of the city has been dated to around 500 BCE. Since no records exist from the city's founding, historians have had to piece together artifacts left behind to gain a better understanding of the city. Around 700 to 900 CE, the city became known for its art. The people of Ife had established themselves as master artisans who created magnificent pieces that became known all throughout the continent and perhaps even farther.

Although few historical records exist, historians theorize that trade played a major role in Ife's economy. Thanks to Ife's advantageous geographical location, the city was able to produce massive quantities of food that could then be traded. The people of Ife had access to yams, dates, palm oil, fish, and okra, which were then transported to North Africa. They also would have exported items such as gold, ivory, pepper, slaves, and kola nuts.

Besides food, Ife's citizens were also master metalworkers. During this period in West Africa, people had begun to work with iron and developed iron-smelting technologies that allowed them to produce high-quality tools and weapons. Their advanced tools helped them to harvest even greater quantities of crops, which would have meant more money for the region and would have ensured that Ife prospered. Besides tools and weapons, the metalworkers of Ife also created artworks that were incredibly detailed.

Glass beads found at Ile-Ife

While Ife wasn't on any direct path that connected to the Saharan trade routes, it made indirect contact with the camel caravans that traveled across the desert. This allowed them to trade goods with communities all over Africa. Eventually, the Saharan trade routes reached as far as the Mediterranean coast, which allowed for better trading opportunities. In return for their exports, the citizens of Ife received luxury and necessary items that they otherwise couldn't produce themselves. Since the city's elite controlled the trade, it's no surprise that many imports included luxury items that probably weren't used by ordinary citizens. Besides salt, which was essential for everyone, Ife's imports included jewelry, perfumes, horses, brass, copper, and swords.

The city thrived on trade for hundreds of years, but historians estimate that the city reached its peak between the 11th and 15th centuries. By that time, it was a massive city with a wall around it and boasted several large buildings. Historians have found evidence of a palace within the city limits, as well as many workshops and shrines. Since Ife was known for being a holy city, it would make sense that it would be the center of worship in the kingdom.

Ife was a true historic urban city, with a system of streets and different sections that would have housed the different social classes. While it's hard to tell exactly what the city was like during its peak, historians have found that the people of Ife were advanced artisans and planned their city well. Several ancient streets were paved with terracotta tiles, which would have prevented erosion and made it easier to navigate through the city.

Many of the homes in the city were built out of clay, which washed away over the years, but the foundations of the homes provide plenty of information for historians. Some of the homes were large and had courtyards as well as several rooms. There's evidence that these homes had private shrines where people could worship their gods whenever they wanted. It's also clear that the people of Ife lived in beautiful homes decorated with ornate designs made out of tiles, pottery, and quartz pebbles. While the walls that held the beautiful designs have long since crumbled, historians are able to piece together some of the designs that once made the homes special.

Unfortunately, the exact reasons behind the fall of the ancient kingdom aren't well known. For some reason, much of Ife's power and wealth shifted to its neighbors, Oyo and Benin, around the 15th century. While the kingdom was erased from existence, the holy city still remains to this day.

Ife: The City of Art

Sometime between Ife's mysterious rise and fall, its residents became master artisans who crafted some of the most beautiful art on the African continent. The city became famous for its art, and the works produced there defined the kingdom's identity. Some of the city's most renowned artworks were life-sized metallic heads. When European travelers saw these, they assumed that the works had come from somewhere else.

According to historians, the heads were crafted in the 11th century and were made using cire perdue, also known as the lost-wax process. This is a process during which a craft wax model is made. Once the model is set, molten metal is poured into the wax mold. The wax eventually melts away, leaving a sculpture behind. Once it's ready, metal pins are put into the core so that the sculpture will hold.

While excavating the city, several life-like metallic heads were found, including some that were made from copper, brass, and ceramic. Like many other aspects of the ancient city, the heads are unique, and they are at the center of an intriguing historical mystery. No one is completely sure why the heads were made or what purpose they served. There are multiple theories, with some thinking that the heads were made to represent gods, rulers, or ancestors. It is also possible that the heads were made for religious purposes or that they were simply made for aesthetic purposes. The heads might also provide an insight into ancient Ife culture, as some of them feature vertical stripes, which could represent scarification. This is a ritualistic practice during which an individual was scarred to signify that they had entered adulthood. However, this doesn't make much sense since the Yoruba aren't known for practicing scarification.

It is also possible that the lines were made for decoration or represented the veils that rulers wore. The heads also feature holes around their mouths, which means that at some point, the statues might have had beads, beards, or veils attached to them.

A metallic head sculpture from Ife
https://commons.wikimedia.org/wiki/File:Yoruba-bronze-head.jpg

While the metallic heads from Ife are unique and noteworthy, the city also produced several other remarkable pieces of art. The people of Ife were adept at making life-like sculptures. One of the most famous sculptures is the figure of a chief wearing necklaces, anklets, a kilt, and a beaded hat and features a double-bow insignia. The chief has a buffalo horn, which may have been used by the ancient people to hold medicine, and a short staff in his other hand.

Several pieces of pottery have also been found bearing geometrical designs and had lids that were sculpted to resemble animal heads. Another intriguing piece of art from Ife is pottery sculptures showing people afflicted with diseases or deformities. It isn't known why these sculptures were created, but they were given human burials.

There were also a number of glass beads at the site, which means that either the people of Ife were expert glassworkers too, or the beads were imported, with Ife's citizens then reworking them. Historians found several ceremonial stools that had been made from quartz. This was impressive because quartz is notoriously difficult to work with since artisans need to grind the stone to get the patterns they want. Unlike other stone materials, quartz can't be sculpted, and the grinding process is long and requires a lot of labor.

The artistic style and methods that were developed in Ife were so renowned that they eventually began to influence the artisans of neighboring kingdoms. Many sculptures and artworks that were uncovered in Benin resembled the pieces created in Ife. At some point in Ife's history, the king sent a sculptor to Benin to share their methods. This ensured that the methods lived on after Ife's mysterious fall.

The pieces found in Ife are some of the most intriguing pieces of art in the world. Although not much is known about the ancient civilization, a remnant of their society will continue to fascinate future generations and stand as a testament to their creativity and incredible skills, thanks to the determined and ambitious efforts of their artisans.

Modern Ife

While it was once at the center of a massive kingdom, Ife is now a city that can be found in the Osun State of southwestern Nigeria. It lies north of Lagos and has a population of over 500,000 people. The city is still a sacred city to the Yoruba people, who make up most of the city's population. Many of the modern people of the city still worship the ancient and traditional gods.

The city is also the present home of the Ooni, who is traditionally the king and spiritual leader of the Yoruba people. The present Ooni was crowned in 2015. Since the city holds important religious significance for the Yoruba people, who make up one of the largest ethnic groups in Nigeria, it is no surprise that the city is the home of several priests and priestesses and the site of religious rituals.

Despite being an ancient city, Ife has modern comforts, such as a maintained road system and constant electricity. The central area of the city is well developed and has homes that are similar to homes all around the world. The city also produces crops, such as vegetables, grain, cacao, cotton, and tobacco. There are also vibrant open-air markets that display the city's spirit as people mingle and shop for what they need.

Due to its age and influence, the city attracts historians and archaeologists who are eager to unearth the secrets of the once-mighty Kingdom of Ife. Multiple excavations have unearthed valuable pottery shards, tools, and pipes. Evidence of iron-smelting and glassworks have been uncovered at Ife and neighboring sites. There's a lot to learn about Ife, and archaeologists are determined to find everything they can. Many of the sculptures and artworks from the region are displayed in the National Museum in Lagos.

While much of the city's influence lies in its status as a holy city, it also has the distinction of being the location of one of Nigeria's best universities, the Obafemi Awolowo University. The university opened in 1962 and was originally known as the University of Ife, but it was renamed in 1987 to honor the influential Chief Obafemi Awolowo, a statesman who played a vital role in Nigeria's independence movement. The city is also home to the Natural History Museum of Nigeria, which draws many visitors.

The Obafemi Awolowo University

Ife started out as a regional town that was built during Africa's early history, but it grew into the massive center of an entire kingdom. It has enjoyed a sacred status for most of its history, which may explain why the city has endured for hundreds of years while other cities crumbled and faded into obscurity. Instead of falling into ruin, it has continued to thrive and has become a modern city that finds itself at the center of a vibrant and dynamic culture.

While it's no longer the capital of a kingdom, it still wields a lot of influence and boasts a lengthy and interesting history. It is still the site of sacred shrines and is one of the most unique cities in the world. Few cities can compare to Ife's age and status. In time, the city's secrets may be uncovered, but in the meantime, it will continue to thrive as a religious and economic hub.

Section 2:
The Age of West African Empires

Chapter 4 – Ghana: Empire of Gold

The ancient Ghana Empire, which interestingly shares almost nothing in common with the modern country of Ghana, was located in parts of the modern-day countries of Mauritania, Mali, and Senegal. Historians aren't precisely sure when it was founded, but the accepted theory is that by the 9th century, Ghana was a force to be reckoned with. At that time, the trans-Saharan trade routes were well established, and trade was one of the most profitable enterprises in the whole continent. Due to camel caravans made up of the Berber people, it was possible to trade all sorts of goods with different parts of the continent.

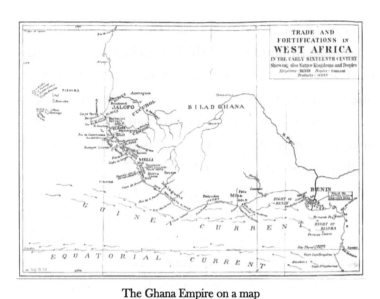

The Ghana Empire on a map
https://commons.wikimedia.org/wiki/File:Map_WestAfrica_16cent_Blake.png

Founded by the Soninke people, Ghana had complete access to the goldfields of West Africa, which meant that it was naturally rich in resources. Soon, the empire had total control of the trans-Saharan gold trade, making it one of the wealthiest kingdoms in Africa. Despite its glittering reputation as the "Empire of Gold," the kingdom is shrouded in mystery but can still offer a fascinating glimpse into a prosperous era.

The Soninke

The Soninke people are part of the Mandé language group who lived in the savannahs between the Niger and Senegal Rivers. They were likely related to the settlers who lived at Dhar Tichitt and its surroundings. The Soninke traveled extensively and formed a link between the Berber people and other kingdoms, which means that they may have played a part in establishing the trans-Saharan trade routes. They were also known for trading gold for salt, which later became a massive component of West African trade.

No one is completely certain how the Ghana Empire was developed, but according to Soninke tradition, they descended from a leader named

Dinga, who came from the Middle East. His son, Dyabe Sisse, formed the kingdom and built Koumbi Saleh, which would later become the capital of the Ghana Empire. This is an interesting theory, but a different Soninke legend suggests that the Soninke originally came from Egypt. These theories aren't taken very seriously by historians, as there is evidence that the Soninke and other similar tribes developed from the societies that occupied Dhar Tichitt and its surroundings.

The Soninke called their kingdom Wagadu, and its current name of Ghana is derived from the title they gave their kings. The word Ghana is thought to mean "warrior king," which sheds light on how the ancient Soninke viewed their rulers or may hint at how their kings took power. The first mention of the Soninke comes from Muslim historians, who credited the Soninke with being the founders of the Ghana Empire.

Over their history, the Soninke migrated through various parts of West Africa, which explains why the modern Soninke people can be found all throughout the region. Today, there are about two million Soninke people.

A 19ᵗʰ-century drawing of the Soninke people
https://commons.wikimedia.org/wiki/File:GuerriersSarrakholais.jpg

Over time, most of the Soninke converted to Islam, which affected every part of their culture. The Soninke also developed a strict social hierarchy that included slaves, who made up the biggest part of the population, and free people, which would have included artisans and tradesmen. This system made it easier for the slave trade to flourish as the trans-Saharan trade routes became more widespread. Since elite families owned slaves, they could get more accomplished, which led to the development of a strict social system that helped turn the Soninke from agropastoral people to the rulers of a wealthy empire.

As the Soninke began trading and mining gold, they discovered that they had an incredible opportunity. Over the course of a few hundred years, their small villages grew larger until they formed a mighty and prosperous kingdom that gave rise to the Ghana Empire.

The Rise of Ghana

By around 1000 BCE, the Soninke had formed small farming communities, which eventually became larger villages that needed to be governed by chieftains. These communities were the first to begin working with iron in the area, which happened around 500 BCE. They needed iron to create superior tools that would help them harvest their crops. Around this time, they made contact with the traders that traveled across the Sahara to exchange their goods.

The Soninke were able to mine iron and gold from their land, both of which were valuable commodities. In time, they were able to build larger towns, and they eventually set their sights on conquering neighboring tribes. This process took time, but by the 10th century, Ghana was a mighty empire with a powerful hold on one of the most profitable trade routes in the world and a wealth of resources in their lands.

When Arab geographer Muhammad ibn Hawqal visited the empire in the 10th century, he was astonished by what he saw. When he wrote a report on the empire, he claimed that the king of Ghana was probably the richest king in the world due to the gold that filled his treasury. Thanks to the Ghana Empire's abundant gold sources and superior iron weapons, it was able to quickly dominate its enemies and become the ruling power in the region. They also had enough money to buy and keep horses, which would have given their army a further advantage. They were also adept at efficient food production, which meant that their economy could flourish.

Historians theorize that Ghana's kings ruled over vassal states that were led by chiefs who controlled smaller portions of land that used to be independent kingdoms or tribes. These chiefs would then pay tribute to the Ghana king. The king of Ghana was also the spiritual leader, which meant that he had absolute power over his people. Along with a well-trained army, this would have been enough to keep his subjects in line. The king also made sure that he was shrouded in mystery. He was always the recipient of sacrifices and religious rituals, and people had to adhere to an austere code of conduct in his presence. When a king died, he was buried in a sacred grove, which was strictly off-limits to anyone else.

The ancient Soninke managed their natural resources well and built up a mighty empire that was known for its wealth. For hundreds of years, Arab scholars described Ghana as the "Land of Gold." In fact, gold was so plentiful in ancient Ghana that ancient scholars mistakenly thought that gold grew out of the earth and that all the people had to do was harvest it as they would any other crop.

One of the biggest reasons Ghana grew into such a wealthy empire is because its rulers recognized the importance of trade and took control of several key trade routes. Evidence of their wealth and power can be found at the historic site of Koumbi Saleh, which may have been the capital city of Ghana.

Koumbi Saleh

When Arab scholars visited the city in medieval times, they encountered a large and prosperous city. In their reports, they estimated that the population of the city was around fifty thousand people, but archaeologists have discovered evidence that the city was probably more numerous than that. The city is also known as Ghana and can be found in the country of Mali. Archaeologists have discovered that the city likely occupied around 110 acres, with smaller settlements on the outskirts of the city.

Koumbi Saleh was surrounded by a massive wall and featured hundreds of homes, a huge gateway, a public square, and a mosque. As with most other houses in ancient West Africa, the houses were made out of dried mudbricks that eventually faded away, leaving behind only the stone foundations. Interestingly, some of the modern inhabitants of the region still use this ancient method of building to construct their own homes.

The city was located in a lush area that yielded plenty of crops for the inhabitants, which would have enhanced the already prosperous economy. Most of the houses in the city were only one story high and were built quite close together. The homes of the elite were bigger, and there are records of the king's palace being surrounded by domed buildings and closed off by a large wall. There were gardens and groves in this enclosed section where priests and religious leaders lived. The kings were also buried in the groves. The city was known as the home of the king, which further gives credence to the theory that the city was the capital of an empire; however, it's possible that the king had residences in other parts of his empire.

Koumbi Saleh occupied an advantageous position on the edge of the Sahara, which would have given it a prime spot on the trans-Saharan trade routes. According to ancient records, the city began as two separate cities, but because people kept building houses in between the two cities, it eventually grew to become one massive city. The first part of the city is known as El-Ghaba, which was where the king and priests lived. The other part of the city was likely a business district since it contained several mosques, which were probably built to accommodate the Muslim merchants. It also had plenty of wells and vegetable gardens where people would have worked.

During its peak, Koumbi Saleh was likely a magnificent city at the center of one of the richest empires in the world. It was also probably where most of the empire's trading took place.

Trade

Trade was one of the most important aspects of Ghana's economy, which meant that the kings of Ghana were determined to keep a firm hold on the gold trade. Ghana exported ivory, gold, slaves, hides, and ostrich feathers to the Berber people (who at this point had adopted Islam as their main religion, which explains why there were so many mosques in Koumbi Saleh's business district). The merchants then took the exports to the north of Africa and beyond. In exchange, Ghana got necessary items, such as salt. The elite in Ghana also imported beads, horses, copper, and textiles. At one point, salt was as valuable as gold, and it was reported that the king of Ghana kept stockpiles of salt in his treasury along with piles of gold.

Gold from Ghana
Cleveland Museum of Art, CC0, via Wikimedia Commons
https://commons.wikimedia.org/wiki/File:Guinea_Coast,_Ghana,_Asante,_19th_century_-_Gold_Weight-_Geometric_-_1962.244_-_Cleveland_Museum_of_Art.tif

The kings of Ghana also knew that gold was only valuable to them if it was rare everywhere else. They went to great lengths to keep the gold trade profitable and even made it illegal to trade gold nuggets, only allowing merchants to trade with gold dust.

Since salt was as valuable as gold, whoever controlled the salt trade had incredible power in their hands. The salt and gold trade were the pillars of the West African economy, and the kings of Ghana relied on this trade to keep their empire wealthy. The relationship between the traders was extremely delicate since the kings of Ghana were determined to keep the extent of their wealth a secret. Around the 10th century, the gold and salt traders took part in something called the "silent trade."

This delicate process meant that the merchants could trade without ever meeting each other face to face and would limit the number of people who saw the gold mines in Ghana. The people of Ghana set a boundary that no one was allowed to cross. When merchants reached the boundary, they would set out the massive salt slabs (salt rocks were transported in bulk). At that time, salt was worth its weight in gold. Once the salt merchants left their wares on the boundary, they would retreat for a day or two. The gold traders would then arrive and leave gold next to the salt. If the salt traders were happy with the amount, they would take the gold and leave. However, if they wanted more, they would leave the gold and salt so that the gold merchants knew that they had to leave more gold. This would continue until the salt traders took the gold, then the gold traders could take their salt, and the deal would be concluded.

The kings also imposed a trade tax on merchants, which meant they had to pay gold every time they entered and left the empire. This would have served the dual purpose of enriching the king and protecting the value of gold.

In time, Islam spread throughout the region, and the empire was undoubtedly influenced by the religion.

Islamic Influence

Since trade was such an important aspect of life in West Africa, many areas came into contact with merchants who brought necessary imports with them. After the Berbers converted to Islam, they took their religion with them and spread Islam wherever they went. This meant that many people came into contact with Islam, and a lot of them accepted the religion and converted.

Since Islam was closely tied to business and trading, some leaders saw the benefit of converting to enhance an already prosperous venture. If they didn't convert, they allowed the Muslim merchants to worship peacefully and even built mosques in their cities. While the kings of Ghana tolerated the Muslim merchants, there's no indication that they converted. Thus, the traditional religion existed alongside Islam. In Koumbi Saleh, there was a massive mosque a few miles away from the royal residence, which was surrounded by traditional shrines. If the kings of Ghana changed religions, they wouldn't have kept the shrines so close to their residence.

While Islam was widespread and continued to be adopted by more and more people, it's clear that Islam only reached the urban areas at first, as the rural communities continued to worship according to the traditional animist religions. When the Muslim traders came to Ghana, they built mosques and brought curious scholars with them who mapped the area and provided reports on what they saw. This means that history that would have otherwise been lost has been preserved for modern historians. These scholars also exaggerated what they saw, which would have cemented Ghana's reputation as the "Land of Gold" all over the world.

It's clear that, at first, the kings of Ghana didn't see a need to do anything more than simply tolerate the merchants' religion. However, as time wore on, it might have been more beneficial if the kings embraced the religion since the two vastly different religions couldn't peacefully coexist for very long.

The Decline of Ghana

An empire like Ghana didn't just fall overnight; instead, it declined over a period of time until it completely fell in on itself. The first serious blow to the foundations of the empire came in the 11th century when the empire's capital was attacked by the Almoravids. This may have been a result of the empire's efforts to control more of the Saharan trade routes. The Almoravids were a force of Berber tribes who were united in their military skill and religious zeal.

The empire never fully recovered from the battle, and it is possible that the Almoravids may have set up their own rulers in Koumbi Saleh, but there's no real proof of that occurring. Over time, the empire began losing strategic trading hubs along the Saharan trade routes, which weakened their control of the trade that once made the empire wealthy. As Ghana lost vital trading points, the Berbers took control of those areas and strengthened their own grip on the Saharan trade routes, which put Ghana at a further disadvantage.

Disaster struck in the 12th century. The empire was forced to endure a prolonged drought, which had a major effect on food production. Meanwhile, other trade routes were established in the east that competed with Ghana's trade routes. Under normal circumstances, these factors would have severely affected a strong empire, but Ghana was nowhere near what it had been. Tensions rose within the government, and a series of civil wars broke out that may have been caused by the two vastly different religions trying to live in the same area. Perhaps if the kings of Ghana had converted to Islam or prohibited the expansion of the religion, they wouldn't have had to deal with civil unrest at that critical point in the empire's history.

During this time, vassal states seized the opportunity to assert their independence, which caused the empire to shrink further. Soon, the empire collapsed, and the Kingdom of Sosso took much of Ghana's territories. Its reign didn't last long; it was soon defeated by Sundiata Keita around 1235 CE, who founded the Mali Empire.

Ghana's Legacy

Medieval Arab geographers traveled extensively and are largely responsible for a lot of the information that exists about Ghana. Abu Ubayd al-Bakri, in particular, recorded plenty of information about Ghana's economy, which still helps modern historians to better understand the mighty empire. Further evidence about the empire was found in the early 1920s when French excavators uncovered Koumbi Saleh, which they firmly believed was the capital of Ghana. Archaeologists continue to excavate sites in West Africa that reveal more about the Land of Gold.

Ghana has always occupied a special place in West African history as the first empire of its kind. In fact, when the Gold Coast gained its independence, the first sub-Saharan nation to break away from colonial rule, its leaders named the country after the mighty Ghana Empire.

Chapter 5 – Mali: An Empire of Culture and Knowledge

The Ghana Empire was the first empire in West Africa, and it was a wealthy powerhouse. However, when it collapsed, it left behind the Kingdom of Sosso, which was quickly defeated by one of the most remarkable rulers in history. Sundiata Keita took control of the region and built a powerful empire by 1240 CE that filled the void left by Ghana.

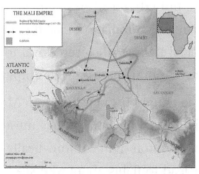

Map of the ancient Mali Empire

Gabriel Moss, CC BY-SA 4.0 <https://creativecommons.org/licenses/by-sa/4.0>, via Wikimedia Commons https://commons.wikimedia.org/wiki/File:The_Mali_Empire.jpg

---

The Mali Empire reached staggering heights that had never been seen in that part of the world. It controlled vast territories, fostered an extremely profitable trading system, and influenced the culture of the region for hundreds of years. Thanks to its compelling rulers, Mali became bigger, richer, and stronger than the Ghana Empire had ever been, and it enjoyed a prestigious reputation in much of the known world. While it eventually crumbled, Mali earned its place in modern memory.

Sundiata Keita

The name Sundiata Keita means "lion prince," which, considering his accomplishments, was probably an appropriate name for the young Malinke prince who would eventually rule much of West Africa. By the time Sundiata Keita was born, the Ghana Empire was a thing of the past, and the Kingdom of Sosso was ruling over a few chiefs who had once pledged loyalty to Ghana. The Kingdom of Sosso was ruled by King Sumanguru, who was known for being a harsh ruler.

Sundiata Keita saw his opportunity and rounded up a few chiefs who were unhappy under Sumanguru's rule and led an army against the Sosso king. In 1235, Sundiata Keita and his army met Sumanguru at Kirina and quickly defeated the harsh king. When Sundiata Keita captured the old capital of Ghana, he set up a government that was comprised of the tribal leaders who had supported him and influential merchants. This government promptly made Sundiata Keita the king. By setting up a central government out of people who were loyal to him, Sundiata Keita was already establishing the foundations for his empire.

Once he was king, he named his new kingdom Mali and set up the line of succession. He ordered that all future kings must come from his clan, but he ensured that the position didn't automatically pass on to the oldest son, which would later lead to fights about who should take control of the throne. He also gave local chiefs a place on his council, a practice that would continue until the empire collapsed.

Sundiata Keita went through great pains to set up a strong internal government that would aid his rule and ensure that his kingdom didn't collapse after he died. While he trusted his advisers with a lot of power, he decreed that only kings should have control of certain aspects of trade and shrouded the royal line with mystical attributes. Unfortunately, by ensuring his own power, he also made sure that the fate of the Mali Empire rested solely on the shoulders of its king, whether that king was competent or not.

The empire's borders continued to stretch as Sundiata Keita conquered neighboring kingdoms. He eventually chose the city of Niani, which no longer exists, as his capital. Once a tribe was conquered, their chiefs were allowed to continue as normal, but they had to pay tribute to Mali. They were also held accountable by a governor who was loyal to the king and who had a small army at his disposal. If there were any doubts about a chief's loyalty, a member of his family would be taken to the capital to ensure that there no rebellions would break out.

Sundiata Keita built a strong empire as he went on conquering territories. He was adamant about making sure that justice was a key feature of his kingdom. People could travel in relative safety throughout the kingdom, and most people had enough to eat. His rule is considered to be Mali's golden age, and stories about his kingdom were told throughout the world. Foreign visitors were blown away by what they saw, and they took stories of the impressive kingdom back with them to places as far as Europe and the Middle East. After Sundiata Keita's rule ended around 1255, he was succeeded by a few average rulers. Fortunately, he wasn't the last good king; in time, Mansa Musa I came to power and began a new golden age for Mali.

Mansa Musa I

Under the reign of Mansa Musa I, Mali would reach its peak and experience greater highs than any other kingdom in West African history.

He came to power early in the 13th century and reportedly had a massive and well-trained army at his disposal. Within a few years, he was able to expand the borders of his empire until it was bigger than Ghana had ever been. Thanks to his efforts, the Mali Empire extended across several countries and included many different cultures. The empire became a melting pot of different people and religions, making it one of the most diverse kingdoms in the world.

Mansa Musa I
https://commons.wikimedia.org/wiki/File:Catalan_Atlas_BNF_Sheet_6_Mansa_Musa_(cropped).jpg

Due to this diversity, Mansa Musa I saw the need to restructure his government. He personally appointed governors over sections of land who would then report back to him and take care of the everyday duties of ruling in that area. The governors would collect tribute and dispense justice. Under Mansa Musa's rule, extensive records were kept and stored in the capital. New territory meant more resources, tribute, and trade opportunities, which enriched Mali beyond belief. Mansa Musa I controlled most of the gold and salt trade in West Africa, and he set up taxes on imports and exports, which made him even more money.

In 1324 CE, he went on a pilgrimage to Mecca, which drew immense interest in the king and his empire. The king brought huge amounts of gold with him on his journey, which he spent and gave away along the way. The king gave away so much gold that the price of gold in Egypt crashed. Stories about the kingdom of gold spread throughout the known world. People imagined that Mali was so rich that the streets were paved with the precious metal and that the people of Mali simply picked it up off the ground.

While Mansa Musa I went through great pains to display the wealth of his empire, he was also a diligent king. He built a number of mosques and Islamic schools in some of his most important cities. Before his reign, the University of Sankoré had been an informal madrasah (Islamic learning center), but the king took a special interest in the school and turned it into one of the best universities in the world. By the time he died, the university's library contained the largest collection of books in Africa, something that hadn't been done since the ill-fated Library of Alexandria.

In 1375, Spanish mapmakers drew the Catalan Atlas, which was one of the first attempts to map the vast region of West Africa. The mapmakers drew Mansa Musa I on the map and gave the king a golden crown. They also drew him holding a piece of gold in his hand. This would have further cemented Mansa Musa's reputation in Europe.

The Catalan Atlas

https://commons.wikimedia.org/wiki/File:Catalan_Atlas_BNF,_sheet_6.jpg

The legends of Mali drew European fortune seekers who searched high and low for Timbuktu, which they believed would help them locate Mansa Musa's gold. While its streets weren't paved with gold, and its people had to work hard to become wealthy, the city of Timbuktu was an impressive trading city during a time when trade was an essential pillar of Mali's economy.

Timbuktu

As with most empires in history, Mali flourished because it occupied a prime geographical region. Its borders reached the Niger River and the Sahara, which meant that they could easily get to the Atlantic coast and trade with the Berber people who ferried goods to North Africa. The citizens had access to various Islamic schools, and the University of Sankoré would have attracted scholars from all over the world. There would have been a wealth of imported goods that would have ensured that the city's elite lived in luxury.

Sankoré Madrasah, also known as the University of Sankoré
https://commons.wikimedia.org/wiki/File:Sankore_Madrasah_in_1893.jpg

Timbuktu was built by the Tuareg people around 1100 CE, and it was eventually conquered by Mali. During its peak, the city would have been a trading hub where valuable goods, such as horses, ivory, textiles, glass, sugar, kola nuts, weapons, grain, beads, art, slaves, and spices, were traded. Mali's elite would have become richer through trading, and the kings of Mali played a massive part in the trade economy.

Mali's kings taxed merchants who transported goods in and out of the country. They also bought goods, raised prices, and made a tidy profit in the process. However, the most important source of Mali's wealth was the gold mines in Bure, Galam, and Bambuk. Gold was extremely valuable since Europeans were beginning to use gold as their currency, which made the gold trade more profitable than it had ever been. Thanks to their monopoly on the gold trade, the kings of Mali could demand whatever prices they desired.

At the Mali Empire's peak, cities like Timbuktu and Gao would have been bustling cities. The ordinary people of the city would have enjoyed a higher standard of living than anywhere else in the empire. Timbuktu was a fabled city that gained a reputation of being one of the most important cities in the world. While Mali remained strong, Timbuktu was like a jewel in the king's crown.

Art and Architecture in Mali

While Mali was rich in several natural resources, stone wasn't something that was common, which presented the empire's builders and architects with a problem. Instead of exporting expensive stones, the builders developed a process of construction that involved reinforcing beaten earth with wooden beams. These beams would often stick out from the walls, creating a unique style. Although many of these buildings didn't survive, some structures, such as the Sankoré mosque, which can be found in Timbuktu, are still standing.

Builders were able to create incredible buildings with multiple stories that would have impressed visitors and foreigners. Mosques were built with massive wooden doors and were beautifully constructed, despite the lack of traditional building materials. Other notable buildings were warehouses, which needed to be big and secure enough to house the goods brought into the city. They also needed to have separate rooms for the merchants who worked in the city. These warehouses were called *fondacs* and could sometimes house up to forty merchants. Examples of these buildings can be found in Djenné, although they are reconstructions to show what they would have looked like.

Mud architecture in Mali
The original uploader was Dario Menasce at English Wikipedia., CC BY 2.5
<https://creativecommons.org/licenses/by/2.5>, via Wikimedia Commons
https://commons.wikimedia.org/wiki/File:Toguna.jpg

Ordinary people lived in beaten earth houses that were reinforced with wood and had a conical roof. While most buildings were made using beaten earth, the rich and elite had more than enough money to import sturdier building materials and constructed their homes out of stone.

The people of Mali had a class of people called griots. These were storytellers and singers who would tell myths and sing songs about heroes and warriors. Music was an important part of Mali's culture, and it would have been especially important during religious rituals. The artisans of Mali, especially at Djenné, were adept at creating sculptures and pottery. These pieces would have been used to decorate homes and shrines.

Malian Sculpture

Sailko, CC BY 3.0 <https://creativecommons.org/licenses/by/3.0>, via Wikimedia Commons https://commons.wikimedia.org/wiki/File:Mali,_figura_seduta,_terracotta,_XIII_sec._02.JPG

Sculptors would create life-like figures, sometimes showing people suffering from disease or kneeling in prayer. Other figures were decorated with beads and depicted soldiers on their horses. It's possible that these pieces were used for rituals, burials, or simply for aesthetic purposes. Since hundreds of sculptures have been excavated, it's easy to imagine that the people of Mali highly prized their sculptures and enjoyed the pieces created by their skilled artisans.

Religion played an important part in Mali's art and architecture. While traditional religions still remained and had an impact on many lives, Islam had a bigger influence on the empire as a whole.

Islamic Influence

As Islam spread through the continent, many African rulers faced an important decision. Since Islam was intricately involved in the efficiency of the trade routes, some African rulers either converted to the religion or tolerated it to ensure the ongoing prosperity of the trans-Saharan trade routes. While the kings of Ghana didn't personally convert, they allowed Muslims to live in peace within the empire. Unfortunately, the tensions between the traditional religions and Islam may have caused the civil wars that crippled the Ghana Empire. Mali took a different approach.

According to Mali oral traditions, the first king of Mali, Sundiata Keita, remained faithful to the old religion, while Muslim scholars claimed that Sundiata Keita was the first Mali king to convert. While there's some dispute over Sundiata Keita's religion, his son, Mansa Uli, went on a pilgrimage to Mecca, and his successors followed his example. Islam became the religion of the royal family, and it's probable that Mali's elite were as well. Islam became widespread throughout the region, but there were still communities that clung to the traditional animist religions.

Mansa Musa I was responsible for spreading Islam on a wider scale. During his famous pilgrimage to Mecca, he brought back scholars and architects to help with his massive building projects. He built the Great Mosque in Timbuktu, as well as many other mosques and schools. Once the schools were built, Mali gained a reputation for having some of the best schools in the world, which, in turn, attracted foreign scholars, especially Arab and Islamic clerics, to Mali's cities. Mali's universities housed thousands of books on every known subject, and scholars could pursue subjects like geography and medicine.

Islam spread as more people converted until generations of West Africans were born into the religion. They studied at the famous universities in Mali or left to study in places like Morocco and became renowned scholars and missionaries. This cemented Islam into West African culture until the religion transformed from a foreign religion into an African one.

However, Islam didn't completely spread throughout the empire. The religion was only taught in Arabic, which would have made the knowledge inaccessible to the uneducated class. The traditional religions were also practiced in rural areas where merchants didn't venture. As time wore on, it became clear that the West Africans worshiped somewhat differently from the Arabs, as they had mixed some elements of their traditional religion into Islam. While Mali's kings were happy to convert, they couldn't risk alienating their citizens by outlawing the native religions. Islam left a definite imprint on Mali's culture, and while the religion may have been good for business, it couldn't save Mali from collapsing.

Mali's Decline

While Sundiata Keita was one of the greatest kings of Mali and created an incredible empire, he may also have inadvertently caused its collapse. By decreeing that future rulers had to be chosen from the Keita clan instead of naming a more specific rule of succession, he caused several civil wars. Influential males within the Keita clan fought for power, which would prove disastrous when Mali faced serious outside threats.

Mali was already failing by the 15th century, and it wouldn't survive as a political powerhouse for much longer after that. As with most influential empires, it attracted powerful external enemies and had to deal with infighting too. The Portuguese had begun opening oceanic trade routes, which spelled disaster for the trading caravans in the Sahara. Gao gained its independence in the 1400s and would later become the capital of the Songhai Empire. In 1431, the Tuareg captured Timbuktu, and other states began to rise up and fight against Mali. By the latter half of the 14th century, the Songhai had become a serious enemy and conquered large parts of Mali.

The last true king of the empire was Mansa Mahmud Keita IV. He ruled over a much smaller kingdom than his ancestors. In 1599, he fought against the city of Djenné, hoping to reclaim its territory for himself. He faced defeat, and Mali was divided into several smaller states. There are legends that say his sons fought for control of his kingdom, but the Mali Empire was long gone.

Mali's Legacy

Mali was a mighty empire that inspired stories of incredible trading cities that housed untold riches. However, archaeology in the region was sparse during colonial times, but in later years, more and more historians flocked to West Africa. They found the ruins of abandoned cities that were once some of the busiest trading hubs in the world. While sites in places like Mesopotamia provided rare and brilliant finds, West Africa had its own treasures to offer.

The Mali Empire once thrived on trade, but recently, a different kind of profitable trade has emerged. The country of Mali legally owns the artifacts discovered on its lands, but elaborate smuggling rings uncover artifacts and sell them around the world. This illegal trade is disastrous, as hundreds of artifacts are lost to these smuggling rings. The government is doing its best to contain the damage.

Some of the cultures that populated Mali still exist and tell stories of their great and prosperous history. During its peak, Mali was one of the most impressive kingdoms in the world, and one of its greatest kings, Mansa Musa I, may have been the richest man in the world, perhaps of all time. With a legacy like that, the legend of Mali will endure for generations. When Mali fell, it was replaced by the Songhai Empire, which went on to become the greatest of all the West African empires.

Chapter 6 – Songhai: Empire of Politics and Power

The third and final West African empire was the greatest of them all. When the Mali Empire fell into political insignificance, Songhai rose to take its place. In time, it would become larger than its predecessors, thanks to the efforts of a gifted warrior king. Unfortunately, unlike the empires that came before it, Songhai wouldn't last for very long. It rose to prominence around 1460 CE, but by 1591, less than two hundred years later, the empire would splinter into smaller kingdoms. These kingdoms squabbled over the scraps that the empire had left behind.

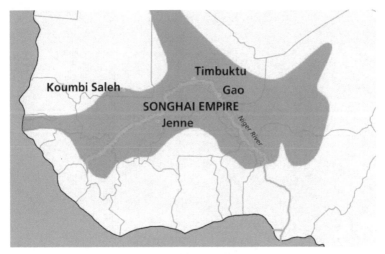

Map of the Songhai Empire

With its capital, Gao, occupying a place on the Niger River, the kings of Songhai were able to take advantage of the trade routes in the area. The empire's kings built a strong central government that kept tight control on key trade cities, such as Djenné and Timbuktu. Songhai's citizens had the distinction of living in one of the most powerful empires in the world. The story of this West African empire begins with a small kingdom on the banks of the Niger River that took advantage of the fall of its predecessor.

Songhai and Mali

The Songhai Kingdom had existed long before it became a formidable empire; it existed at the same time as the Ghana Empire. Its capital was Gao, which was founded around 800 CE. Thanks to its position along the banks of the Niger River, the city enjoyed a flourishing economy and handled luxurious goods from all over the continent. It was almost as important as Timbuktu. However, when the Mali Empire rose to power, the kings of Mali set their sights on the trading city in an effort to keep tight control of the trade routes in the region. For hundreds of years, Gao existed as a vassal state that served the Mali Empire, but the Songhai people weren't willing to fully submit to their Malian overlords. They regularly rebelled against Mali and repeatedly attacked Malian cities.

When Mali declined in power, the Songhai took their chance. In 1375, the people claimed their independence and separated from the empire. Not only was the kingdom free from Mali, but the Songhai also started conquering large pieces of the empire, which enlarged their borders. In 1465, the Songhai defeated Mema, and in 1468, they took Timbuktu, which the Tuareg people had recently captured.

The decline of the Mali Empire allowed the Songhai Kingdom to go from a mere vassal state to a strong regional power in its own right. With their capital at Gao, the Songhai were able to claim the profits of the trade in that area, which enriched their kings and strengthened their army since they could more easily import horses for their warriors. The acquisition of Timbuktu only made them stronger since it was one of the largest and most profitable cities in West Africa. As Mali lost more and more of its territories, the once incredible empire was split up into smaller, more insignificant kingdoms that fought amongst themselves for what little power was left.

The more Mali retreated, the more land the Songhai were able to conquer. However, the Songhai weren't the only enemies that Mali faced. They also had to fight off the Tuareg people, who came from the Sahara, and the Mossi people, who wanted more control of the Niger River. Soon, Mali only had some of its western lands left, which they managed to keep until the Moroccans invaded in the 17th century.

While the Songhai were able to establish themselves as a mighty kingdom, it wasn't until King Sunni Ali came to the throne that Songhai began reaching its full potential.

Sunni Ali

For most of the Songhai people's history, they relied on launching small, repeated attacks on their neighbors. While this worked for a while and won them some territory, it wouldn't be enough to create an empire. All of this changed when Sunni (also spelled as Sonni) Ali Ber came to power. There are many conflicting theories about his life, but one thing is certain—he was an incredible military leader. He presented himself as a man of the people and mixed Islam with traditional religions, which allowed him to have a foot in both camps.

Instead of relying on guerilla tactics, he introduced campaign warfare. From then on, the Songhai went on prolonged military campaigns and conquered large portions of land that greatly expanded the borders of their kingdom. King Sunni Ali was the first great king of the Songhai Kingdom, and he was determined to rule an empire.

Not only did Sunni Ali change the Songhai people's tactics, but he also armed his warriors with some of the best weapons in the region. He commanded a formidable cavalry and controlled a massive fleet of ships that he used to defeat territories along the banks of the Niger River. Before long, he controlled much of the land that used to belong to the Mali Empire. He also gained a reputation for never losing a battle, which would have struck fear in the hearts of his enemies, making it easier to conquer them.

He also used the traditional religions to his advantage by claiming that supernatural animist forces were on his side, which would have effectively scared many of his enemies. As he swept through West Africa, he set up a central government, chose governors, and exacted tributes from defeated chiefs. While he engaged in a lot of warfare, he also improved the infrastructure of his new lands, which would have benefited the locals and ensured the continued prosperity of his empire.

Sunni Ali became known as "Sunni the Merciless," as he attacked territories with stunning speed and sheer force that caught his enemies unaware. If a territory proved to be cooperative, he would incorporate their men into his army, but if a tribe or kingdom resisted him, he wouldn't show any mercy. Muslim chroniclers, in particular, portray him as a violent and cruel leader. He apparently turned against courtiers on a whim and executed thousands of people. When the Fulbe tribe proved to be difficult to subdue, he promptly executed the entire tribe. Slaves also had fewer rights under his rule and were forced to fill a quota of grain. Their children were also slaves from birth. According to Islamic chroniclers, he killed and drove Muslim clerics out of Timbuktu when he conquered the city.

While Islamic chroniclers had a dim view of Sunni Ali, traditional legends were somewhat kinder. According to oral traditions, Sunni Ali was a powerful magician, and he was forced to retaliate against the Muslim elite of Timbuktu when they wouldn't allow him to take his troops over the Niger River. Whether or not Sunni Ali was a cruel man, he was one of the greatest kings of the Songhai Empire. In fact, he was responsible for establishing the empire. He died in 1492 after fighting the Fulani, but there are rumors that he was poisoned by Muhammad Ture, the man who would eventually take the throne for himself.

Muhammad I

Not much is known about Muhammad Ture's early life, but oral tradition claims that he was Sunni Ali's nephew. According to that same tradition, Muhammad's mother was Sunni Ali's sister, and his father was a jinni, a powerful supernatural being. This mystical origin story might have developed long after his death, and it would have cemented his powerful reputation.

There are rumors that Muhammad Ture murdered Sunni Ali, but those reports can't be confirmed. After Sunni Ali died, his son, Sonni

Baru, ascended the throne. Sonni Baru was crowned in January 1493, and Muhammad Ture was already trying to usurp the throne a month later. Things came to a head in April 1493 when Muhammad Ture's and Sonni Baru's troops met in battle. Muhammad Ture won the throne and changed his title to Askia, which became the title used by all his successors.

While Sunni Ali was a warrior king, Muhammad focused on setting up an efficient government. He appointed ministers of justice, protocol, agriculture, forests, and finance, which would have ensured that the daily affairs of the empire ran smoothly. The army and navy were also reorganized so that the men were under a capable general and admiral. Most of these positions were filled by his family members, which would have consolidated his dynasty. He also divided the empire into manageable provinces and chose trustworthy governors to keep the peace and enforce justice.

During Sunni Ali's reign, a mix of traditional religions and Islam existed, but Muhammad I converted to Islam and was a deeply religious man. He even went on a pilgrimage to Mecca. During his pilgrimage, he imitated the example of the Malian kings and displayed his wealth during his journey. Due to his religious vigor, he also received the title "Caliph of Sudan." He encouraged Arab scholars and architects to return with him to his empire, and education flourished in his capital city.

When he returned from his pilgrimage, he was ready to expand Songhai's border. Unfortunately for him, he was a better statesman than a warrior. Although he managed to conquer some territories, he lost quite a few battles, and he had to deal with several rebellions and revolts during his reign. His influence stretched throughout the region, and he dreamed of making his empire the ideal Islamic state.

As the king aged, his children began fighting amongst themselves for power, much to his dismay. In 1528, Muhammad I was exiled, and his son, Askia Musa, took the throne. Within three years, Askia Musa was assassinated by his brother, who then became king and imprisoned Muhammad I on a small island in the Niger River. By 1537, one of his other sons, Askia Ismail, deposed his usurper brother and brought his father home. Muhammad I died in 1538 and was buried in an elaborate tomb that still exists to this day.

Muhammad Askia I's tomb in Gao

Taguelmoust, CC BY-SA 3.0 <http://creativecommons.org/licenses/by-sa/3.0/>, via Wikimedia Commons https://commons.wikimedia.org/wiki/File:Askia.jpg

Before he died, he gave his son, Askia Ismail, his saber in gratitude for bringing him home. Due to his reputation as a deeply religious man, his tomb is home to one of the most famous mosques in the world.

Gao

At its peak, Gao had a population of over 100,000 people. The king of Songhai ruled from Gao and had absolute power over the people. There were at least seven hundred eunuchs at court at any given time, but the Songhai royal court was a dangerous place. Most of Songhai's rulers were killed by their uncles or brothers during the never-ending fight for power.

Boats on the Niger River in Gao

Albert Backer, CC BY-SA 3.0 <https://creativecommons.org/licenses/by-sa/3.0>, via Wikimedia Commons https://commons.wikimedia.org/wiki/File:GaoPirogeNiger1990.jpg

The capital city was also the home of the imperial council. Thanks to Muhammad I's efforts, the Songhai had a much more efficient government than those of Ghana and Mali. If a king survived long enough to rule, he could rely on the help of senior officials. Besides the inner council, there were ministers who dealt with trade, wages, property, and agriculture. There were people who kept the peace, collected taxes, and dispensed justice. All these officials kept the empire running while the royal family fought for control.

Gao was also an important trading city like Timbuktu. Unfortunately, Songhai didn't have access to the goldfields of the Gold Coast since the Portuguese had secured their interests in the region. However, the Songhai were able to control the trans-Saharan trade routes, which funneled valuable items into the empire. The trading cities of Songhai received cloth, glass, sugar, and horses, and they exported hides, slaves, spices, ivory, and kola nuts,

While Songhai didn't have the same vast gold reserves as Ghana and Mali, it managed to become rich despite this disadvantage. Thanks to this, Songhai's most important cities were the epitome of urban living. Most houses in the trading cities were built from stone. The cities also had mosques and Islamic schools, which promoted education within the empire. The people who lived in the outskirts of the trading cities usually built their houses out of mud or lived in tents. Timbuktu, in particular, thrived as a learning and religious center.

Gao was at the center of the empire, and its citizens enjoyed the advantages that came along with that status. While the Songhai Empire thrived, so did the city, but since the city's fate was tied with the empire's, it meant that when Songhai fell, so did Gao.

Songhai Religion

At the beginning of the Songhai Empire, Islam and traditional religions existed side by side. This was due to the fact that Sunni Ali worshiped however he saw fit. When it was convenient, he adhered to Islamic traditions, but he also observed animism practices. He actively made sacrifices to traditional gods and seemed happy to blend the two religions together. However, if any Muslims opposed him, he retaliated violently. For a long time, Islam had been the religion of the educated elite, but Sunni Ali went to great pains to present himself as a man of the people. And the people preferred their traditional religion.

In stark contrast, Muhammad I was a deeply devout Muslim convert who made the pilgrimage to Mecca. While he was an accomplished statesman, his religious fervor may have caused his downfall. He tried to make Islam the empire's official religion and chose Muslim judges to occupy important positions in the government. Soon, the government's elite were almost completely Muslim, and a scholarly class developed within the empire. Muhammad I rejected any attempts to blend the religions, but he was unable to convert everyone in his empire, which was a sore point for him. By establishing a version of Islam that wasn't mixed with traditional elements, Muhammad I gave the impression that Islam was a new religion, which caused people to view it with suspicion. When his dreams failed, he became a bitter old man who caused many of his children to despise him. While he was a capable leader for most of his life, he was forced to watch as his children fought and killed each other to claim his throne at the end of his reign.

The educated populace of the empire was largely Muslim and worshiped according to the Islamic law, which was enthusiastically enforced by Muhammad I. Urban cities housed scholars who studied the religion and various other subjects, further enforcing the idea that Islam was a religion for the upper classes.

However, the people who lived in rural areas clung to their traditional beliefs. This was largely due to the fact that Islam was inaccessible to them; in addition, their beliefs were tied to their surroundings. They believed that every object had a tangible spirit that had an effect on their surroundings, especially the spirits Harake Diko (spirit of the Niger River) and Dongo (associated with thunderstorms). These spirits required constant sacrifices, which meant that the traditional religions required intensive labor. Dead ancestors were also appeased with food, drink, and elaborate ceremonies that involved masked dancing. Much of their art also reflected their traditional religions.

Songhai straw necklace

While Islam flourished in urban areas, the majority of the empire continued to worship according to the ancient traditions, much to Muhammad I's dismay. Unfortunately, his successors had bigger problems to deal with.

The Decline of Songhai

King Muhammad I was the last great king of Songhai, and after his reign, the empire fell victim to several civil wars. Songhai slowly shrank in the second half of the 16th century. By 1586, Mohmmed IV Bano and his brothers divided the kingdom and weakened it during a critical time in Songhai's history. During this time, Morocco was looking for a way to take over Songhai territory to gain control of the trans-Saharan trade routes. In 1591, Sultan Ahmad I al-Mansur Saadi of Morocco sent a relatively small force of four thousand men to capture the empire. The opposing forces met at the Battle of Tondibi, where the last king of Songhai, Askia Ishaq II, made his final stand.

While Songhai's army vastly outnumbered the Moroccan forces, the Moroccans were armed with muskets and cannons. This was the first time that Songhai's army encountered such advanced weaponry, and they were completely defeated. Askia Ishaq II was killed by Morocco's allies, and Morocco was left with a massive territory.

Unfortunately for the Moroccans, Songhai proved to be a difficult region to rule. They were unable to suppress the near-constant rebellions that broke out. Morocco had invaded Songhai because it hoped to take over the profitable gold trade, but it found that its goal was beyond its grasp due to logistics. Eventually, the Moroccans left Songhai, but the empire was unable to regain its former glory. For the next few hundred years, various leaders would try to restore Songhai, but they were unsuccessful. The French would conquer them in 1901.

Songhai's Legacy

The Songhai culture still exists in modern-day Niger and the western Sudanic region, and they are primarily a Muslim community. They are split into several sub-groups and have a rich, vibrant culture. Archaeologists are still discovering secrets of the empire that once ruled most of West Africa and are amazed by the artifacts found at the old sites. Meanwhile, the modern Songhai people still live in the same bend of the Niger River and cultivate the land.

Modern Songhai pottery
C. Hugues *https://www.flickr.com/photos/chugues/*, *CC BY-SA 2.0*
<*https://creativecommons.org/licenses/by-sa/2.0*>, *via Wikimedia Commons*
https://commons.wikimedia.org/wiki/File:Songhay_pottery_gorom_gorom_market.jpg

Songhai was the last of the pre-colonial West African empires, and it was certainly the greatest. It was larger than the other two and thrived despite the lack of the illustrious gold mines that enriched its predecessors. While it only existed for a little over a century, it left a lasting impression on African history and boasted some of the most capable kings that Africa had ever seen. Its rise was meteoric, and its collapse was disastrous, but at its peak, it was one of the greatest empires of its time.

Section 3:
The Spread, Decline, and Impact of European Imperialism

Chapter 7 – The Transatlantic Slave Trade

The slave trade was already a part of West African history by the time Europeans reached African shores. These slaves were used for their labor or skill and were a part of many West African societies. However, the transatlantic slave trade grew when Europeans trafficked African slaves across the Atlantic to the American colonies from the 16th to 19th centuries. It was the largest slave trade in history, and over twelve million people were taken from their homes to work in foreign territories. The transatlantic slave trade formed part of the triangular trade, which involved taking slaves from Africa to the Americas, coffee and sugar from the Americas to Europe, and textiles, wine, and ammunition from Europe to Africa.

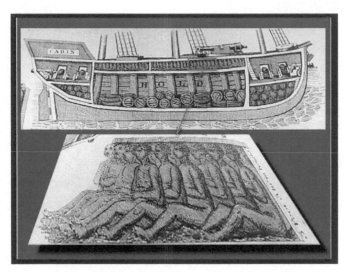
A slave ship used during the transatlantic slave trade
https://commons.wikimedia.org/wiki/File:NavioNegreiro.gif

The slaves were supplied by West and North African leaders who brought the slaves to trade cities, where they were then loaded onto European ships. The slave trade existed within trade routes that had developed over the centuries. Europeans brought items, such as cloth, guns, beads, and ammunition, which they exchanged for slaves. The slaves were forced onto massive ships and lived in deplorable conditions for weeks as they headed toward an unknown destination.

The slave trade had disastrous consequences for the African continent, especially for West Africa, which contained some of the busiest slave-trading ports.

The Rise of the Slave Trade

Slavery had been a part of Africa's trade economy long before the Europeans ever reached African shores. However, those early slaves were prisoners of tribal wars and made up a slave class within African societies. They played a role in building and strengthening the communities that they served. The transatlantic trade essentially drained a huge region of necessary communities that could have built up economies and developed the resource-rich lands of Africa for the benefit of Africans. Unfortunately, for a couple of hundred years, people were transported across the ocean to work for the benefit of foreign powers.

The Portuguese set the foundations of the slave trade in the 1400s, as they took African slaves from West Africa to work on sugar plantations in the eastern Atlantic. At first, they simply purchased the slaves who were already being traded in West Africa. However, as their need increased and the demand for slaves couldn't be met, they traveled farther inland and captured slaves themselves. They soon found that this was a difficult undertaking, especially when Portuguese troops lost miserably to Senegalese warriors in 1444. After that, they decided to strike bargains with African leaders who supplied the necessary slaves.

By 1502, the Spanish got involved in the slave trade and took Africans to the Caribbean. While the Spanish conquistadors played a part in the slave trade, the Portuguese still controlled the main operations.

The slave trade proved to be very profitable, and soon other European powers wanted to get involved. In the 1600s, the Dutch controlled much of the slave trade. However, the British and French soon took the lead, and by the 1700s, they were in charge for the most part. Most of their trade originated from the shores of the Niger and Senegal Rivers. As the demand for slaves increased, European powers found that they needed to do more than just trade with African leaders. They approached certain African tribes and offered them financial incentives to fulfill the demand for slaves. European leaders gave certain tribes money and ammunition against their enemies. The more conflict they generated, the more slaves they got in exchange. Unfortunately, this further destabilized an already failing region.

West African Slave Ports

As certain parts of West Africa began trading with Europeans, they were named after their main exports. As a result, the Gold and Ivory

Coasts became world famous. Unfortunately, the Slave Coast also earned its name the same way. West Africa's coast exported a myriad of beautiful items, but soon its main export was slaves. There were many slave ports that existed along the coast. One such port was on the island of Gorée in Senegal. The island is a small piece of land made out of volcanic rock and has the distinction of being one of the first European settlements. Thanks to its position off the Cape Verde Peninsula, it was the ideal spot for Portuguese traders.

Slave House, Gorée
Robin Elaine, CC BY 2.0 <https://creativecommons.org/licenses/by/2.0>, via Wikimedia Commons https://commons.wikimedia.org/wiki/File:Senegal_Gor%C3%A9e_(8).jpg

When the Portuguese arrived, they set up various buildings and forced the indigenous Lebu people off the island. It was an active slave depot for most of the slave trade, and many of the buildings used by the slave traders still exist and have been preserved or turned into museums. The island was declared a UNESCO World Heritage Site in 1978 and attracts many visitors who want to catch a glimpse into the island's history. One of the most famous buildings is the Maison des Esclaves, or Slave House, which has several displays on slavery and many artifacts from the era. It also contains the aptly named "Door of No Return," where slaves would pass through to board slave ships. What was once a source of horror for countless slaves is now a beautiful little town controlled by the Senegalese government, which put a lot of effort into preserving the memory of the slave port.

Elmina Castle, located in modern-day Ghana, was one of the most important slave ports on the West African coast. It was declared a UNESCO World Heritage Site in 1979 and receives thousands of visitors every year. At first, it was an important location for trading gold between Africa and Europe, but like Gorée, it served a darker purpose during the slave trade. It was used to test captives to see if they were healthy enough to be sold, and the various dungeons were usually full of people waiting to be transported across the ocean. Modern visitors are taken on a tour of the castle and are able to get an idea of what captives went through before they were loaded onto the slave ships. Like at Gorée, Elmina Castle has a Door of No Return, and the castle looms over a lively little town that still pays respect to that dark period in its history.

Another famous slave port is located in Badagry, Nigeria. At first, the camp was used for trading items like palm oil, but by the latter half of the 1600s, it was an important part of the slave route along with Calabar. Slaves were marched along the coast until they reached Badagry, where they would then be forced into slave cells called barracoons. One such barracoon still stands and is used to display artifacts used during the slave trade.

This barracoon belonged to Seriki Faremi Abass, a former slave who was allowed to return home on the condition that he worked with his former owner to facilitate the sale of slaves at Badagry. He soon became a famous slave merchant in his own right. Abass used to sell slaves in exchange for household items. Since the Europeans wouldn't accept local currency, slaves were used as currency, and he famously exchanged forty slaves for an umbrella. He also bought cups, records, and other items, sometimes for ten slaves each.

Seriki Faremi Abass Museum in Badagry
https://commons.wikimedia.org/wiki/File:Seriki_Faremi_Abass_Slave_Museum_,_Badagry_03.jpg

Like Gorée, Badagry is now the home of several slave museums that exist to showcase the stories of the people who were taken from their homes and forced to build the New World or serve in foreign plantations.

The Middle Passage

The Middle Passage was a stretch of the Atlantic that went from Africa to the slave ports in Brazil or the islands in the Caribbean. Slaves were forced to march from the interior of West or Central Africa, where they had been captured, to one of the various slave ports that dotted the West African coast. From there, they were packed onto ships. The conditions aboard these slave ships were inhumane, and an estimated 1.8 million died crossing the Middle Passage. The voyages lasted for weeks and crossed about eight thousand kilometers (five thousand miles). Oftentimes, slaves would have to endure months aboard the slave ships.

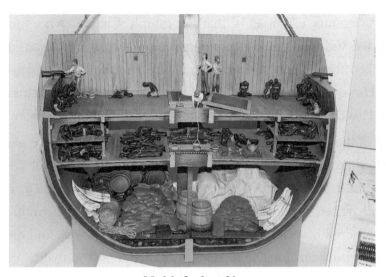

Model of a slave ship

Since the slave trade was primarily focused on profit, slaves were tightly packed onto the ships without any regard for comfort or sanitation. The ceilings were very low, which meant that the slaves couldn't sit up and were forced to lie flat on their backs for most of the day. The bottom of the slave ships was terribly hot, and disease was rampant. It was also hard to breathe because oxygen levels were so low. According to reports, oxygen was so scarce below deck that they weren't able to light any candles. Slave merchants also reduced the amount of time that slaves were allowed on the upper decks because captains were afraid of mutiny. The longer the voyage, the more slaves died. However, by the 1800s, the voyages had become much shorter, which resulted in fewer deaths.

However, slaves weren't the only ones to die during the brutal voyages. The unsanitary and crowded conditions caused deaths among the crews that helped transport the slaves. Captains and merchants also had to be fairly careful with the slaves since they were only paid for the number of live slaves they delivered. Sometimes, the slaves were able to capture slave ships. A famous example is that of Joseph Cinqué, who was being transported with fifty-three other captives aboard the *Amistad* in 1839. They killed the captain and crew and were eventually allowed to return home. However, these revolts were rarely successful, which means the Middle Passage wasn't the source of hopeful stories about liberation.

One of the most shocking reports from the Middle Passage happened in 1781 when Captain Luke Collingwood caused the death of 130 men, women, and children aboard the *Zong*. Somewhere during their travels, a passenger picked up an infectious disease that spread like wildfire. The captain ordered that all the captives be thrown into the sea, and once they reached their destination, he filed an insurance report so that he could be compensated for his lost cargo. Unfortunately, during the slave trade, the life of a person had a price tag.

The Life of a Slave

With the exception of those who were born into slavery, slaves started out as people who were part of West African tribes. Usually, they were attacked by warlords who had been bought off with European weapons. Once they were captured, they would be forced to march to the coast. The journey wasn't easy since they had to traverse difficult terrain while chained to another person, with chains on their ankles and rope around their necks. As the slave trade continued, the warlords traveled farther into the interior of the continent, which meant that a trek toward the coast could be as long as 485 kilometers (300 miles). Hundreds of people died along the way.

Once they got to the port, they were kept in barracoons or slave castles, such as Elmina or the Slave House on the island of Gorée. They were then inspected to see if they would survive the journey across the Middle Passage. The slavers would count the captives' teeth and force them to jump to test their agility. Once a captive passed the test, they were led to a dungeon or housed in a barracoon. The dungeons were ghastly places;

they contained dark rooms with straw on the floor and a bucket for captives to relieve themselves. Sometimes they would have to wait for months before they were shipped off to a new destination. Merchants would negotiate the sale of the slaves, and once the negotiations were completed, they would brand the slaves before loading them onto the waiting ships.

A slave-holding cell in Elmina Castle. This cell could hold up to two hundred slaves.
Kurt Dundy, CC BY-SA 3.0 <https://creativecommons.org/licenses/by-sa/3.0>, via Wikimedia Commons
https://commons.wikimedia.org/wiki/File:Ghana_Elmina_Castle_Slave_Holding_Cell.JPG

Whatever horrors were faced en route to the slave ports were nothing compared to what slaves experienced on board the slave ships. And once the slaves reached their destination, they were sent off to work. Most slaves ended up on plantations and faced grueling work under inhumane conditions. They were forced to work six days a week, from dawn to sunset. Worst of all, they often had to work under brutal overseers who let their power go to their heads.

Some slaves were managed by drivers who were former slaves. Drivers were despised for obvious reasons, and this often led to conflict and tension. A slave's welfare depended largely on their master. If their owner did well, then they could expect regular meals, but if a slave worked for a small landowner, they had to hope for good crop yields. Domestic slaves had somewhat easier lives and were regarded as being "better" than plantation slaves. This distinction led to the formation of a social hierarchy within the slave ranks.

As the slave trade developed, so did slave codes, which were rules that differed from region to region. These codes dictated the treatment and laws that applied to slaves. For example, the education of slaves was illegal, and marriages between slaves weren't legally binding, which meant that families could be split up on a whim. The slave codes are shocking examples of how badly slaves were treated. Besides the brutal impact that slavery had on individual lives, it also spelled disaster for the African continent.

The Slave Trade and West African Cultures

Europeans weren't able to capture enough slaves on their own, and their early ventures into the African interior to capture slaves were disastrous. They were forced to work with several African leaders to gain the necessary number of slaves. In the beginning, the slaves were mostly captives of political battles, but in time, warriors traveled into West and Central Africa with the sole purpose of capturing slaves. There was no way for captives to bargain with these men, and entire tribes were wiped out to be sold to Europeans.

By the time the Europeans reached African shores, West Africa was already divided into kingdoms and states that regularly fought each other for control of trade routes and prosperous regions. Those early European explorers could buy slaves from any African port since the slave trade was already established into the identity of many West African kingdoms. However, when the demand for slaves increased, the Europeans had to get creative. They negotiated agreements with some African leaders and brought luxury items from Europe to ensure that the African leaders continued trading with them.

A 19th-century drawing of African captives marching toward the coast
https://commons.wikimedia.org/wiki/File:Slaves_ruvuma.jpg

While Europeans profited greatly from the slave trade, they were subject to the terms set by African rulers. There were several instances when the African leaders decided not to trade their slaves. Unfortunately, the longer the slave trade went on, the more the African leaders were subjected to European demands. The more slaves were transported out of the continent, the fewer people were left to strengthen African armies and economies.

It's difficult to know the precise impact that slavery had on West African cultures since some cultures suffered more than others. Some West African kingdoms used the slave trade to their advantage by getting rid of their political rivals. However, some regions, such as parts of Guinea, had to be avoided because the people strongly resisted the slave trade. As slavers decimated certain areas to get more slaves, some towns fought back. The people fortified their towns and set guards to alert the people if slavers approached.

Slaves also resisted long after they were taken away from their homes. There were many reports of serious rebellions. Some slaves would go on hunger strikes on slave ships. Others would jump from the ships so that they wouldn't have to live as slaves. On plantations, the slaves would sometimes revolt and take their overseers as prisoners. Although millions of people were forced into slavery, many of them fought back and refused to submit to their fate.

While some West African cultures benefited from the trade, it was still a brutal practice that dehumanized millions. And for most regions, the ban on slavery couldn't come soon enough.

The Ban on the Slave Trade

Not everyone supported slavery, and there were several movements to abolish the practice. However, abolition efforts didn't really start to take hold until the American Revolution. While many people opposed slavery, there were still some who argued that the practice was necessary for the American economy. The subject divided the northern and southern colonies of North America. The first country in the Western Hemisphere to abolish slavery was Haiti, which did so in 1804. It wasn't until 1808 that the US slave trade was abolished. Unfortunately, an illegal slave trade developed, which meant that more slaves were still smuggled into the country. On top of this, slavery itself wasn't abolished. These practices would continue until after the end of the American Civil War in 1865.

Great Britain had ended its slave trade in 1807. In 1833, it outlawed slavery in most of its colonies. From that point, Britain sought to stop the transatlantic slave trade and actively sent their navy out to stop slave ships and illegal smuggling. Brazil followed suit with ending the slave trade in 1850, but slavery didn't stop in the country until 1888. As the slave trade declined, many parts of Africa were destabilized and vulnerable. Unfortunately, European leaders took advantage of that fact, and the Scramble for Africa began.

Chapter 8 – The Scramble for Africa

For much of its history, Africa remained a mystery to Europe. It was nicknamed the "Dark Continent" because virtually nothing was known about the people and the land. As intrepid explorers began traveling Africa, they discovered that the continent had a vibrant mix of cultures and was rich in resources. As the slave trade began dying down, it became apparent that Africa had a lot to offer by way of natural resources.

African map of European colonies

The potential for European colonies became clear once King Leopold II of Belgium set up a colony in the Congo region. Soon, European leaders were locked in a mad rush to secure their own colonies. All of this came to a head in 1884/85 when thirteen European countries and the United States met at the Berlin Conference. At the conference, they set up the rules for dividing Africa into colonies. The lines drawn on the African maps showed little regard for ethnic or geographical factors but soon became real borders that split families. The colonialization of Africa had severe consequences, as tensions about Africa's division would contribute to the First World War.

While West Africa was just emerging from the horrors of the slave trade, it was further destabilized when foreign powers descended onto the region to claim its riches for themselves.

The Pre-Colonial European Presence in Africa

Hundreds of years before the Scramble for Africa, Europeans had made contact with the African continent. During those early years, they didn't have much success penetrating the interior of Africa, but they set up trade routes and built forts to protect their interests. As the slave trade progressed, more contact was made with various parts of the continent. European countries mostly had contact with coastal communities and didn't have much to do with African tribes who lived inland.

Britain's presence was confined to parts of Sierra Leone, the coast of Gambia, and the Gold Coast. France controlled some parts of Dakar, Senegal, and Côte d'Ivoire. They had already begun the process of colonizing Algeria, but their presence would only be firmly established after the "Scramble." Portugal and Spain also had interests in Africa, but before the Scramble for Africa, Europe controlled less than 10 percent of the continent.

The European fascination with Africa was reflected in the number of explorers that flooded the continent in the 1800s. One of the most famous explorers was David Livingstone, who went on several difficult expeditions. He managed to map much of South and Central Africa, during which he found famous sites like Victoria Falls, which had previously been named Mosi-oa-Tunya. During the 1800s, a new expedition was sent to Africa almost every year, and the farther explorers ventured into the continent, the more they realized that Africa was a rich land.

David Livingstone
https://commons.wikimedia.org/wiki/File:David_Livingstone_-1.jpg

Other famous expeditions were conducted by James Grant, John Speke, and Richard Burton. In fact, it was John Speke who located the source of the Nile. Exploration was encouraged by the African Association (founded in London in 1788), which wanted to find the legendary city of Timbuktu. Ever since the days of Mansa Musa I, the city had gained a mythical reputation, and the banks of the Niger River received hundreds of visitors who wanted to find the city with untold amounts of gold. At first, the exploration of Africa was inspired by scientific inquiry and curiosity, but as explorers came back with stories of the riches contained within the continent, greed became a definite factor.

Soon, rich Europeans were financing expeditions so that explorers could bring back accurate reports of economies and resources. The Industrial Revolution ensured that Europeans would be able to expand, and they were looking for opportunities to do so. In time, a number of factors would contribute to the invasion of Africa.

The Cause of the Scramble

Unsurprisingly, most of the causes of the invasion of Africa originated in Europe rather than Africa. As reports of Africa's wealth flooded in from explorers and missionaries, the general public's curiosity was aroused. For hundreds of years, European leaders had their eyes on how to expand their interests on the continent, and they soon found that the road to invasion was finally opening up.

Meanwhile, explorers found that they had more access to parts of Africa, especially with the use of steam engines and iron-hulled boats. Livingstone used a steam engine when he traveled on the Zambezi River. Once he reached land, he had the steam engine taken apart and carried to Lake Nyasa, where he resumed his travels. The invention of the steam engine changed the world of trade forever, as travel became faster and more efficient. Future explorers like Henry Stanley and Pierre Savorgnan de Brazza would follow Livingstone's example and use steam engines on their expeditions.

Henry Morton Stanley, in particular, played a large part in the Scramble for Africa. After he returned from an exploratory mission, he reported that Africa had vast natural resources that were ripe for the taking. King Leopold II of Belgium employed the explorer to set the stage for a Belgian colony. Henry Morton Stanley returned to the Congo area and began making treaties with local chiefs on behalf of Belgium. It wasn't long before other European powers followed suit.

Henry Morton Stanley
https://commons.wikimedia.org/wiki/File:Wr_Studio_Portrait_of_Henry_Morton_Stanley,_ca._18 90,_published_by_L_Herbst.jpg

When the transatlantic slave trade ended in Europe, various African and Arab merchants were still enslaving people since the practice was an essential part of their economies. Various activists were disgusted and wanted to ensure that slavery would be finally abolished all over the world. Britain was actively part of the fight against slavery, but in many ways, their efforts simply weren't enough.

However, the end of slavery also caused a gap in the European economy, which needed to be filled. Explorers returned with fantastic reports about ivory, gold, sugar, timber, and other profitable resources. Having given up slavery, merchants were looking for legal ways to keep up with trade, and the explorers' accounts gave them a reason to reinvest in

Africa. However, Europeans reasoned that the best way to protect their interests would be to set up colonies. The only problem was that many of their past efforts to set up colonies failed, partly because of the African diseases that were fatal to European explorers.

Malaria and yellow fever had long been a problem for Europeans on African shores. The majority of Europeans died within their first year of setting foot in Africa. In 1817, two French scientists found a cure for malaria by extracting quinine from the cinchona tree. This allowed Europeans to better survive in Africa, which revolutionized trade and exploration.

The invasion of Africa was becoming increasingly attractive to European leaders, but a few more things had to develop first. By the 1800s, Europe was becoming too small for European leaders, and Germany, Britain, and France kept pushing for power and dominance. When Africa opened up, the solution to their problems was clear. However, a land grab was only worth the effort if they could conquer the civilizations that already existed in Africa. Unfortunately for Europe, African kingdoms had been armed by Europeans for hundreds of years during the slave trade. If their armies fought each other, there was a big chance that the Europeans would lose badly and would be worse off than before.

Everything changed in the 1860s when percussion caps and breech-loading guns were introduced. Percussion caps combined gunpowder, bullets, and wadding and were waterproof, which allowed Europeans to transport them much more easily. Breech-loading rifles fired faster than older muskets and could be loaded while lying down. African leaders were armed with old muskets that loaded slower. They also had to be loaded while standing up and required vast amounts of gunpowder, which wasn't waterproof. Europeans monopolized these new weapons and kept them from the Africans, which gave them a decided advantage in the coming land grab.

Breech-loading rifle
Greener, W. W. (William Wellington), No restrictions, via Wikimedia Commons
https://commons.wikimedia.org/wiki/File:The_breech-loader_and_how_to_use_it_(1892)_(14586474470).jpg

After the Industrial Revolution, Europeans viewed technology as an indication of civilization. Since Africa hadn't gone through its industrial revolution yet, the people were viewed as uncivilized. This gave Europe its final excuse to invade Africa. European leaders claimed that they wanted to help Africans and turn them from savages into enlightened people. However, the truth was that Europeans wanted Africans to work on plantations and produce profitable crops that would boost Europe's ailing economies. By the 1880s, Europe was rushing headlong into Africa with boundary markers. It soon became a messy fight, and the need for strict laws became apparent.

The Berlin Conference

During the 1880s, European countries rushed to Africa to set up their own claims and lay the foundations for their colonies. Soon, the French set up treaties with the local people north of the Congo River, and a year later, they set up a protectorate in Tunisia. The British took control of Egypt in 1882, and in 1884, France and Britain created Somaliland. In the same year, Spain and Germany claimed their own lands. However, this rush led to tensions that could have exploded and caused massive wars. A solution was needed, and in 1884/85, European and American leaders met to discuss ground rules for the invasion of Africa. Unfortunately, no African leaders were invited to take part in the conference.

The result of the conference was the General Act of the Berlin Conference. The various European powers agreed that anyone was allowed to travel on the Congo and Niger Rivers and that if a country wanted to create a colony, they had to be able to run the colony effectively. Borders were drawn on a map, and European countries began claiming African land as their own.

A political cartoon of the European leaders at the Berlin Conference
https://commons.wikimedia.org/wiki/File:Cartoon_depicting_Leopold_2_and_other_emperial_po
wers_at_Berlin_conference_1884.jpg

However, a lot of work was required to enact the visions of the European leaders. First, they had to build infrastructure in the regions they invaded. They had to buy steamships to navigate the rivers and build railroads that could carry people and resources into their new lands. It was difficult for European powers to rule their colonies at first because the new borders didn't take into account the different ethnic groups, some of whom proved to be very difficult to govern. Once the Europeans arrived, they tried to take over the local trade but experienced some rebellions, which made them realize that they didn't understand the people they were trying to rule.

African groups, such as the Fulani, Tuareg, Asante (Ashanti), Opobo, and Shona, fought against the European invaders. Unfortunately for them, they were soon subdued by the European armies, which had superior weapons. It wasn't long until most of the continent was made up of European colonies. Liberia and Ethiopia were the only countries that remained independent during this period. Liberia was the home of many former slaves who were sent away from the United States after the abolishment of slavery. Since Liberia was part of the declaration to abolish slavery in the United States, it was prevented from claiming it as a colony, although some see it as an informal colony. Meanwhile, the Italians tried on numerous occasions to claim land in Ethiopia, but the Ethiopians strongly resisted these attempts. In 1896, the Italians were defeated by the Ethiopians and forced to retreat. The Italians did eventually claim Ethiopia for a few years, but their control didn't last long.

Meanwhile, most of Africa was being invaded and forced to work for European colonists. A lot of colonists resorted to violence to keep control of their new regions, and the invasion allowed atrocities to be committed against the native civilizations. The most notable example was King Leopold II's crimes against humanity in his personal colony in the Congo region. For instance (and this is just one example of many), if the

Congolese failed to meet their rubber quotas, their hands were often cut off as a punishment. Meanwhile, West Africa was forced to yield to British and French invaders.

British West Africa

Britain controlled several territories in West Africa. These countries included Gambia, Nigeria, the Gold Coast, Sierra Leone, and British Togoland. The British developed a system of indirect rule. They divided their territories into manageable regions that were overseen by a governor who was advised by a council. Traditional rulers were allowed to keep a measure of power so that they could take care of judicial decisions and the administration. A British officer was usually appointed to facilitate relationships between the colonial and traditional governments. Unfortunately, colonial governments usually removed Western-educated African leaders from their positions and prevented any changes or developments in traditional governments.

In 1787, Sierra Leone was colonized by Britain after freed slaves were sent back to Africa from England, Nova Scotia, and Jamaica. At first, the colony was controlled by a private company called the Sierra Leone Company, but the colony was declared a crown colony by Britain in 1808.

The next British colony was Bathurst, which was located on the banks of the Gambia River. Sierra Leone and Bathurst were both created to help the British combat slavery, but the British soon moved inland and enlarged their colonies. Eventually, Britain went on to colonize parts of the Gold Coast. Some parts of the Gold Coast held out for as long as possible. The Asante Empire was only conquered around 1900, and in time, its ruler was allowed to resume his duties under the British system of indirect ruling.

Britain's colonies increased after the First World War, as the League of Nations decreed that Germany's colonies had to be divided between Britain and France. As a result, Britain got parts of Togoland and

Cameroon (Kamerun). After the Second World War, the United Nations set up trusteeships that prevented European powers from governing colonies with absolute authority. For the first time, the colonies were allowed a voice on the international stage. The United Nations Trusteeships ensured that colonies would be supervised by a trust country that had to answer to the Trusteeship Council so that conquered territories could be allowed to recover. It wasn't long before the British colonies began to claim their independence.

French West Africa

French West Africa was also known as French Afrique-Occidentale française, and it included the countries of Senegal, the Ivory Coast, Sudan, Dahomey, Mauritania, Haute-Volta, and French Guinea. The French ruled over their colonies from 1895 to 1958.

Map of French West Africa
https://commons.wikimedia.org/wiki/File:Britannica_French_West_Africa.png

The governors of French West Africa reported directly to the minister of colonies, who lived in Paris. Each colony had a governor who would report to the governor-general who was based in Dakar, Senegal. The governor-general would receive his orders from the minister of colonies and communicate with the rest of the governors. In 1946, the Grand Council of French West Africa was formed, which consisted of the governors of each colony and a member of the French population from every colony. The council met in Dakar and served to help the governor-general.

Meanwhile, the people were governed by Cercle commanders. Cercles were made up of subdivisions that were easier to govern. Cercle commanders often had thousands under their control, and they would have to answer to district commanders. Cercle commanders had a lot of power over their citizens and were allowed to judge, punish, or imprison the people. The citizens of Cercles were also subject to the whims of their commanders. If a new commander was appointed, he was allowed to shuffle the affairs of the Cercle as he saw fit. The French colonial governments also appointed local chiefs to oversee the ordinary people. These chiefs were chosen based on their service and devotion to the French government without any regard to the traditional rights of power.

The Impact of the Scramble for Africa

By the time the Scramble for Africa ended, European powers controlled one-fifth of the globe's land, and by 1914, Britain controlled almost 30 percent of Africa's population. In Europe and elsewhere, the general public was convinced that the colonies were a force for good due to extensive propaganda. As territories were conquered, indigenous people were brought back to inform and entertain the general public. These exhibitions were immensely popular and led to the formation of several human zoos in London, Hamburg, Antwerp, Milan, New York, and Warsaw. Scientific studies of the time were meant to dehumanize Africans, with prominent Darwinists and scientists with racist ideologies claiming that certain African tribes were the missing link in evolution.

These racist ideas helped to legitimize the Scramble for Africa and any other atrocities that were reported. Missionaries were sent to Africa to convert the natives to Christianity, which reinforced the idea that the colonists were helping Africans become "civilized."

Meanwhile, in Africa, the effects of the "Scramble" were much darker. The colonial governments subjected many of their citizens to forced labor as they built railways and cities. However, most native people were forced to work on plantations under inhumane conditions to produce cash crops. Traditional governments were destabilized, as the ancestral rights to power were ignored so that colonial lackeys could be put in positions of power. Social movements were quickly suppressed, and educated African leaders were often removed from their positions.

At first, many cultures tried to fight back, but they were quickly subdued by the European armies. When groups tried to rebel later on, they were punished, and entire tribes were wiped out or separated. Thousands died after being exposed to European diseases, and they completely lost control of their land. Traditions were lost forever as colonists changed laws and enforced European ideals. Although European countries did everything they could to keep their colonies, African leaders began to declare their independence as soon as they were able.

Chapter 9 – The Surge of Independence

Ever since European countries began to colonize Africa, they believed that Africans needed help and that it was their moral right to subdue the countries and bring them under European guidance. However, it quickly became apparent that colonialization only benefited Europeans. Due to extensive and often racist propaganda, the general European public believed that the colonies were a good thing. And then the First World War broke out.

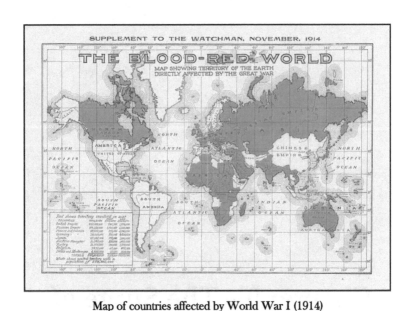

Map of countries affected by World War I (1914)
https://commons.wikimedia.org/wiki/File:The_Blood-
Red_World_Map_Showing_Territory_of_the_Earth_Directly_Affected_by_the_Great_War.jpg

Everything changed after the Great War. The general public became disillusioned with their rulers and began to realize that the colonial system had to be readjusted. Changing attitudes in Africa led to a surge of countries claiming their independence between 1957 and 1976. Unfortunately, these independence movements were often met with strong resistance, and violent conflicts broke out around the continent. However, the colonized African countries were determined to gain their freedom back, no matter the cost, and in time, they were finally free.

Changing Views in Europe

The First World War brutally swept through Europe between 1914 and 1918, causing about forty million deaths worldwide. By the time the war ended, the people knew the world would never be the same. In the face of such unprecedented carnage, radical ideas began to emerge. People began rejecting traditionally held beliefs, as they had seen for themselves that the old systems simply didn't work. Among other things, people began to question whether or not European countries had any right to rule African countries.

After the war, the League of Nations set up a series of mandates that would dictate how the German colonies would be divided and how they should be run. Unlike other colonies, these conquered colonies wouldn't become the possession of whichever country colonized them. Instead, the British and French were given the responsibility of helping the African countries develop their own governments. It was the first step toward independence, but there was still a long road ahead.

League of Nations emblem used at the 1939 World's Fair
Martin Grandjean This W3C-unspecified vector image was created with Inkscape., CC BY-SA 4.0
<https://creativecommons.org/licenses/by-sa/4.0>, via Wikimedia Commons
https://commons.wikimedia.org/wiki/File:Flag_of_the_League_of_Nations_(1939).svg

In 1929, Britain enacted the Colonial Development Act, which allocated British funds toward the development of their colonies. It was a relatively small amount, but it was supposed to help the indigenous people build up their own systems to generate income. However, just a year later, the world entered the Great Depression. Suddenly, tens of millions of Europeans and Americans (as well as people from many other countries) were left without work, and the world's economy stalled. People were desperate for solutions, and all eyes turned to Africa.

People began to realize that if the Africans were allowed to manage their own affairs, they could become rich in their own right and spend money, which would then stimulate the world's economy. However, for that to happen, the reigning colonists had to loosen the reins somewhat. The idea was that Europeans would help their colonies produce more resources, which would, in turn, help the European economy regain its strength. It was becoming increasingly clear that Europe had begun to rely too heavily on its African colonies. This caused friction as they aimed to exploit more of Africa's natural resources. The First World War had been a direct result of European leaders' failings, and Africa had been dragged into a bloody war that sapped its resources. As tensions rose, disaster struck in the form of the Second World War, which would be a turning point in the struggle for independence.

The Impact of World War II

World War II proved to be much worse than the Great War, and the entire planet felt the war in one way or another. While only parts of North and East Africa were subjected to living through battles on its lands, millions of Africans were drafted into a war that had almost nothing to do with them. It was the second time in less than fifty years that their supposedly more civilized counterparts subjected them to a brutal war that wouldn't otherwise have affected them. The war was difficult and cost many lives, but African leaders were paying close attention to military and leadership tactics, which would aid them in their fight for independence.

One of the reasons that Europe was able to colonize Africa so completely was because Africa was divided and fell victim to infighting. During the Second World War, many African cultures fought together against a common enemy, and they learned a vital lesson. If Africans wanted to claim their independence, they had to fight together. The foundations for the fight for independence had been set.

When the war ended, Africans everywhere were shocked and offended when they received little to no recognition for their efforts in the war. They had lost much and fought hard against Adolf Hitler's forces, but they weren't given awards or commended for what they had done. Millions of Africans were deeply offended, and their anger would give them the motivation they needed for the fights ahead.

Meanwhile, in Europe, the war had shattered an already fragile economy, and Europeans had to deal with the fact that they weren't invincible. The Allied forces had won the war, but it had come at a great cost. European leaders had to focus on fixing things on their own shores, but their colonial governments were struggling greatly as well. The war had impoverished many communities, which led to civil unrest that the colonial governments couldn't handle on their own.

Nationalism was at an all-time high all around the world. The Second World War had revolutionized the concepts of race and freedom. Hitler and his racist regime had exterminated millions of Jews, as well as millions of other minority groups and prisoners of war. The world was horrified. With the Atlantic Charter, Britain's prime minister and United States' president promised that once the war was over, they would respect the right of all peoples to live under their chosen form of government. These promises resonated with people all over the world.

In Asia, nationalism was succeeding, and they were overthrowing their colonial governments, which inspired many African leaders. Anti-colonial ideas were becoming popular, and the United Nations reflected these views. The formation of the Trusteeship Council allowed Africans to complain against their colonial governments and gave them a platform to be heard. World War II had proven that Europe was not undefeatable, and as their power declined, the United States and the Soviet Union became world powers that supported anti-colonial views. Due to all of these factors, the age of European imperialism was coming to a dramatic conclusion.

Liberia

Liberia is a fascinating country for a number of reasons, but one of those reasons is that Liberia is one of only two African states that were never fully colonized, with the other being Ethiopia. It's also Africa's oldest republic and was the first African country to elect a woman, Ellen Johnson Sirleaf, as their head of state. The country was established in 1821 by the American Colonization Society and was the home of many repatriated slaves. In 1847, Liberia claimed its independence and was a relatively stable country until a rebellion in 1989 that led to a civil war that lasted until 2003.

Liberian flag
https://commons.wikimedia.org/wiki/File:Flag_of_Liberia.svg

The country boasts naturally rich biodiversity and beautiful landscapes that became the home to many immigrants over the centuries. The three major groups are the Americo-Liberians (immigrants from North America who became the ruling party for much of Liberia's history), indigenous people who lived in the country before the American Colonization Society procured the land, and West African immigrants who fled slavery and the colonial governments. The country is a melting pot of cultures, and while English is the main language, more than twenty languages are spoken within the country's borders.

The capital city, Monrovia, was founded in 1822 and has been the center of the country's development ever since. It is located on Cape Mesurado and has breathtaking views of the Atlantic. It is home to various ethnic groups, including the Vai, Kpelle, Loma, Dan, Mano, Mende, Malinke, and Ngbandi.

During the 1400s, Portuguese sailors landed on Liberia's coasts and quickly discovered that the area was rich in Melegueta pepper, which was as valuable as gold for some time. This area became known as the Grain Coast. When the abolishment of slavery became a serious topic, Americans began looking for a good home for former slaves, and Liberia seemed like the best option. Treaties were made with local chiefs that allowed the freed slaves to build themselves a home. The state was founded by Jehudi Ashmun, who left Liberia in 1828. At that time, Liberia had laws, trade, and an effective government, and in 1841, Joseph Jenkins Roberts became the first black governor. Under Roberts, the country became an independent republic.

Joseph Jenkins Roberts

While it experienced a turbulent history, the country kept its independence and has managed to survive a series of destructive civil wars that threatened its existence.

Prominent West African Leaders

While Britain and France tried to prevent African leaders from gaining too much power in their colonies, there was still a system of education in place in the colonies. Christian schools were allowed to teach some of the native citizens, but this education wasn't widespread and easily accessible. Britain and France also had to give some native people positions of power. By the latter half of the 1900s, universities had opened in Dakar, the Gold Coast, and Nigeria. This led to a small but educated class of African people who had their own political ideals. Unfortunately, they weren't given many opportunities within colonial governments, which meant that they had the knowledge and ability but no political power. They came to realize that they couldn't use their skills to benefit their people while under colonial rule. However, once independence became a real possibility, several leaders were ready to take charge.

Kwame Nkrumah on Ghanaian memorial stamp

Kwame Nkrumah was a prime minister of the Gold Coast. He became the first prime minister of Ghana and then the president of the Republic of Ghana. When he was a boy, he lived with his family in a rural area and attended a Roman Catholic school. He did well academically and was able to attend Prince of Wales College and School in Accra. He eventually attended universities in North America and the United Kingdom. While in the United Kingdom, he became a co-organizer of the 5th Pan-African Congress.

When he returned to the Gold Coast, he founded the Convention Peoples' Party (CPP), which became one of the leading voices for independence. He was imprisoned for his activities, but the Convention Peoples' Party won the elections in 1951, and he was elected as prime minister. He was incredibly popular among his people for most of his term as prime minister, and he invested heavily into the country. However, his presidency, which he obtained in 1960, eventually became authoritarian. He was deposed in 1966.

Léopold Sédar Senghor

Léopold Sédar Senghor was the first president of Senegal and is known for being a poet and philosopher. He was born in a small coastal town and attended a Catholic school in Dakar. He pursued additional education in France and lived as a French citizen for some time before he was drafted into the French Army. When he returned to Africa, he joined several political parties and served as the deputy from Senegal in the French National Assembly. He was instrumental in helping Senegal join the Sudanese Republic, which formed the Federation of Mail. At that time, he became the president of the federal assembly. In 1960, Senegal became a separate country, and he became its first president. He served his country until he resigned in 1980 and died in France at the age of ninety-five.

Ahmed Sékou Touré
https://commons.wikimedia.org/wiki/File:Sekou_Toure_usgov-83-08641.jpg

Ahmed Sékou Touré was the first president of Guinea and served in his post for thirty years until he died in 1984. He was born into a rural family and wasn't able to pursue much education. He worked as a postal clerk but became involved in a trade union. This was the beginning of his political career, and soon, he was actively advocating against colonialism. He became the leader of the Parti démocratique de Guinée and was instrumental in rejecting the new French constitution, which led to Guinea's independence. He became Guinea's first president. As with other African leaders of the time, he was strongly influenced by socialism and Marxism.

Ghana

On March 6th, 1957, the Gold Coast became an independent state, one of the first African states to do so. The leaders of the country decided to find a new name for themselves, and they settled on Ghana, which was the name of the first great West African empires. Under the rule of Kwame Nkrumah's CPP, Ghana was ready for a new future. Nkrumah's supporters became almost cult-like, and he was given the title "Osagyefo," which is the Akan word for "redeemer."

Nkrumah dreamed of creating a socialist Africa and wanted to help other African countries gain their independence. As time went on, he took more power for himself and his political party, which ultimately led to his downfall. Unfortunately, independence was a difficult undertaking, and by 1966, Nkrumah was struggling under weighty foreign debts, a corrupt government, and increasing poverty. He was replaced by Lieutenant General Joseph Ankrah of the National Liberation Council. Ghana struggled as power changed hands numerous times during its history, but it has successfully held a number of democratic elections.

Guinea

On October 2nd, 1958, Guinea gained its independence from France under the direction of Ahmed Sékou Touré. In time, Guinea made trade agreements with China and the Soviet Union, but due to Touré's authoritarian regime, the economy wasn't able to flourish. It soon came under heavy foreign debt, as the government struggled with the adjustments needed to become fully independent from France.

Touré struggled to rule the country, and after facing a lot of rebellions, difficulties, and conspiracies against his authority, he became paranoid, which led to him keeping a tighter hold on his power. While his popularity soared during the early years of his rule, when he died, his party found that they had little support from the general public. His successor, Colonel Lansana Conté, ruled the Military Committee for National Recovery. Unfortunately, during his rule, Guinea fought against Sierra Leone and Liberia and had to deal with political unrest. In time, the presidential term was shortened, and in the last decade, Guinea has made real economic progress.

The Year of Africa

In 1960, seventeen African countries gained their independence. This year has become known as the "Year of Africa." In West Africa, the countries of Togo, Mali, Benin, Nigeria, Burkina-Faso, Côte d'Ivoire, Senegal, Nigeria, and Mauritania took advantage of the winds of change and claimed their independence. This mass movement was made possible because of the Algerian Revolution, which forced France to help many of its colonies become independent. Britain followed France's example to prevent a war of their own, as they had enough to deal with already.

As independence swept through the continent, African nationalism was at an all-time high, and many countries began the long process of becoming stable under their own rule. Independence movements led to radical changes that revolutionized Africa. Cape Verde gained its independence in 1975, making it one of the last West African countries to do so, and it marked the end of European imperialism and colonialism in this region.

While it was a long journey to independence, it was well worth the sacrifices that needed to be made along the way. Many countries struggled for decades to gain stability since they had to learn how to manage their wealth and recover from the exploitation of their labor and resources. The effects of colonialism cannot be accurately measured, as many countries are still feeling the effects, but many former colonies are gaining their footing and making an impact on the global economy. While many countries struggled under repressive regimes and corruption, in time, they will be able to become great in their own right. The age of West African empires proved that Africa has a lot of potential, and it's that potential that many West African leaders are hoping to harness.

Chapter 10 – Traditional Cultures and Religions of West Africa

West Africa is a melting pot of interesting cultures and religions. Each ethnic group has its own traditions that were impacted by its history and location. Since West Africa covers an extensive region, it would be difficult to catalog all the different cultures, but thankfully, many of the cultures intersect with each other and have a few things in common.

One must remember that these cultures are still unique, though. Some share a common religion, with the people practicing Christianity, Islam, or traditional religions that have ancient roots in Africa. West Africa is the home of several intricate and vibrant cultures that have survived incredible circumstances.

Edo

The Edo people of Nigeria have a rich history and were once part of the Kingdom of Benin, which ruled territory west of the Niger River. Many of the Edo people are either Muslim or Christian, but there are still some who believe in the traditional religion. According to the traditional religion, there exists an omniscient god named Osanobua. There are also several lesser gods and spirit beings who interact with the supreme god on behalf of humans. The worshipers of this traditional religion are required to leave behind offerings to please their gods. They also have shrines dedicated to individual gods or spirits. A lot of Edo art is distinctive since their works represent their unique belief or events in their history.

Bronze leopards found in Benin
Rolf Dietrich Brecher from Germany, CC BY-SA 2.0 <https://creativecommons.org/licenses/by-sa/2.0>, via Wikimedia Commons
https://commons.wikimedia.org/wiki/File:Bronze_Leopards_from_Benin_(26475275146).jpg

The modern Edo people live in villages and towns in Nigeria (as well as elsewhere around the world), and their villages are run according to a strict system. The head of the village also serves as the priest and is usually the oldest male in the community. In the past, the Edo were ruled by a sacred king. Older men in the village will usually act as a council to run the village efficiently. The younger men will help the village council or take care of difficult tasks in the community. And finally, the younger boys are tasked with easy but necessary labor, such as taking care of communal buildings.

The Edo culture includes skilled artisans who carve wood, cast bronze, weave clothes, and work with leather. Their traditional attire is beautiful and includes red beads, jewelry, and body markings.

Akan

The modern Akan people can be found along the coast of Guinea and speak a number of languages, including Asante, Baule, Anyi, Fante, and Guang (among others). Many Akan people live in Ghana, Togo, and Côte d'Ivoire. Their traditional religion includes ancestor worship, as well as the belief in a supreme deity who is served by lesser beings. However, most Akans are now Christians, and only a fraction worship the traditional ways. Akan art is known around the world and includes using bronze and gold weights. Over the years, Akan culture reached many different parts of the world, which means that Akan stories, names, and languages can be found in the Caribbean, as well as in the Americas.

An Akan weight for measuring gold dust

Muséum de Toulouse, CC BY-SA 4.0 <https://creativecommons.org/licenses/by-sa/4.0>, via Wikimedia Commons https://commons.wikimedia.org/wiki/File:Akan_MHNT.ETH.2010.25.121.jpg

In the 15th century, the Akan people controlled some of the most prosperous gold mines in Africa, which made them a very powerful group and brought them into contact with European traders. When colonialism began to spread, the Asante, in particular, fought against European invasion and managed to hold out for a considerable period of time before they were defeated and colonized.

The Akan are traditionally matrilineal, which means that genealogy is traced back through their mothers. Although there are many different groups of Akan people, they consider themselves to be one nation. Each family line has its own god, and the head of the family is usually in charge of the stools that represent the unity between the ancestors and the living family members. Each group also has its own rules of etiquette and rituals.

The modern Akan people live in villages, where the inheritance of land is determined based on matrilineal traditions. The head of the village is usually elected to his position and is supported by a council. The villages are usually divided into family lands, where extended families live and take care of each other.

Yoruba

The Yoruba are one of the largest groups in Nigeria, but some of the Yoruba people live in Benin and Togo (as well as elsewhere in the world). The modern Yoruba people are mostly farmers, with men growing crops such as millet, peanuts, beans, and corn, among others. While the men work in the field, the women are usually in charge of markets, and social status usually depends on a woman's place in the markets. While many Yoruba people work on farms, they also have skilled artisans. Yoruba artisans are considered some of the best in Africa, and they work with glass, iron, ivory, and wood. Other crafts include weaving, spinning, dyeing, and basket-making. Their traditional clothing is usually brightly colored and features geometric designs.

While the Yoruba people have a lot in common, like their language, they were divided into separate kingdoms during their long history. Some of the Yoruba royal lines still exist but aren't as influential as they once were. Each village falls under a chief and his council. The Yoruba are a patrilineal society, which means that inheritance is determined according to the father's lineage. Most villages have their own gods, taboos, and traditions that were developed through several patrilineages.

Many modern Yoruba people still worship according to their traditional religion, but the practices of the traditional religion can differ according to their region. They believe there is a supreme god with lesser divinities that can be called on for help. The deities don't have set identities and can be worshiped differently according to where their worshipers live.

Family relationships are very important to Yorubas, as is the concept of a best friend. In the Yoruba culture, best friends see each other every day, and when a person is about to die, they entrust their best friends with instructions about what to do after they have died.

Serer

The Serer people are one of the largest ethnic groups in Senegal but can be found in Mauritania and Gambia. Most of the Serer are farmers and work with crops like millet, rice, and livestock. The modern Serer people still live in villages that are grouped according to their family lines. They have a matrilineal society. Marriages are often arranged, and a groom is required to produce a bride price, which is usually paid with livestock. In villages where men have more than one wife, the wives commonly have their own homes in the husband's compound.

In the past, the Serer heavily resisted conversion to Islam, but modern-day Serers are predominantly Muslim. In the 19th century, they fought violently against conversion attempts, but soon, they had to fight against the invading French. Once they lost against the French, many Serers converted to Islam. A small fraction of the Serer population still practices the traditional animism religion, and some have become Christians. One of the most famous Serers was Léopold Senghor, who became the first president of Senegal.

The Serers also have an interesting history. During medieval times, they ruled several kingdoms, including the Kingdoms of Saloum and Sine. These kingdoms were ruled by Serer patriarchs who even took control of Wolof kingdoms, such as Baol and Cayor. While not much is known about their kingdoms, they were once powerful people who controlled much of the region and fought against invaders with everything they had.

The Serer culture managed to survive much turmoil, and the modern Serer people enjoy a rich culture that places a high value on family life.

Igbo

The Igbo culture is one of the most famous African tribes, thanks to their entrepreneurial efforts. They have many fascinating traditions that have survived throughout many hundreds of years. According to Igbo mythology, the culture was founded by Eri, who was sent down to Earth to create civilization. Eri is a famous figure in Igbo tradition, and it has been theorized that Eri was the son of Gad, who was mentioned in the Bible.

While the modern Igbo people live in the region of Igboland, which was founded along parts of the Niger River, there are also Igbo people in Guinea and Cameroon. However, like with many other African people groups, parts of their culture have ended up all around the world, including Jamaica, North America, and Cuba.

Igbo traditional clothing

Jibofoto - NATHANIEL AJIBOLA, CC BY-SA 4.0 <https://creativecommons.org/licenses/by-sa/4.0>, via Wikimedia Commons https://commons.wikimedia.org/wiki/File:Nathaniel_Ajibola_Igbo_Woman_Nigeria.jpg

They have many unique traditions, including their wedding customs, which take place in stages. In the Igbo culture, the prospective groom must visit his bride's father to get his blessing. Then the groom will bring his family to meet with the bride's extended family, which also must consent to the marriage. On the third visit, he will have to pay the bride price. It's during this stage that the bride's family will hand the groom a list of items that he must deliver before the wedding. Once the groom passes all the stages, the couple's friends and family will gather together. The groom will then hide among the guests, and the bride must find him to give him a cup of wine before the wedding can begin. Many Igbo traditions highlight the importance of the family unit and respect for elders.

The modern Igbo people are mostly farmers, but many of them are accomplished merchants and artisans. Crops are an important part of the culture, and yams are their staple food. The Igbo people celebrate the festival of Iri Ji, which is the New Yam Festival. It highlights the importance of the crop.

Malinke

The Malinke (Mandinka) people can be found in various West African countries, including Liberia, Guinea Bissau, Sierra Leone, the Ivory Coast, Senegal, Mali, and Gambia (also known as The Gambia). Most of the Malinke have descended from the Mali Empire, which was one of the greatest empires in history. After the empire fell, the people scattered to different regions, with some remaining in the regions that the old empire occupied. When the Portuguese landed on African shores, they enslaved some of the Malinke people. Soon, the Malinke made up a sizeable portion of the slaves who were traded during the transatlantic slave trade. However, the Malinke also provided slaves that were captured during battles.

Most modern Malinke people are Muslim, and most of their villages have a mosque. Due to their religion, many of their customs conform to Islamic traditions, but some traditional rites still remain. One of the most prevalent rites is circumcision, and there are also puberty rites that determine the privileges of adulthood and marriage. Boys are usually taken from society about eight weeks before their circumcision, which usually happens between the ages of eight and twelve. During this time, they are trained. Girls are usually only trained for about two weeks and receive their circumcision around this time too. During this training, young Malinke children are taught about the Malinke culture. In recent history, many people have tried to put a stop to female circumcision, which is also known as female genital mutilation. However, some communities won't stop the practice.

Marriage ceremonies are usually a source of great joy in Malinke communities. A girl is usually betrothed at a young age. Once she is ready for marriage, the groom will pay a bride price to her father. A bride price usually consists of salt, kola nuts, and livestock, which were historically paid to fathers during Malinke history, but money is also acceptable.

Wolof

The Wolof people can be found in parts of Gambia and Senegal and are predominantly Muslim. For much of West Africa's history, they were an influential community that lived along the coast of Senegal. They are traditionally farmers who work with sorghum and millet, and their villages are usually run by a chief. Wolof artisans are adept at working with gold, fabric, and wood. The Wolof people are also known for their keen business sense, and while they are firmly established in West Africa, they can be found in different parts of the world.

The Wolof are so influential that while Senegal's official language is French, most people can speak Wolof. Their language is spoken in various parts of West Africa. For most of their history, the Wolof observed both patrilineal and matrilineal practices, but since most Wolof people are now Muslim, they're mostly a patrilineal society today. Their culture values hospitality, and impromptu visitors must be invited to share a meal or stay the night. While Wolof people who live in urban areas enjoy modern comforts, the people who live in rural areas still use some ancient traditions in their daily lives. For example, traditional healers still use spells and herbs to treat their patients.

While the Wolof dress similarly to other Senegalese cultures, Wolof women are known for their flamboyant styles and are often seen with intricate hairstyles, jewelry, and dresses.

In the Wolof culture, naming ceremonies are very important, and choosing a name for a child is a serious responsibility. Usually, parents choose to honor close friends or family members by naming their children after them. Once a boy is eight years old, he is assigned to an older male who will teach them about Wolof traditions. The older male is called a Selbe, and it is his duty to guide the boy to manhood. It's usually around this age that the boy is circumcised.

Age is greatly respected among the Wolof people, and special care is given to older family members, who are valued for their wisdom. As with many other West African cultures, family is extremely important to the Wolof.

West African Vodun

Vodun (also spelled as Voodoo, Vodou, or Vodoun) comes from the Fon language of Benin, which means "spirit." It evolved in Haiti after West African slaves were transported to Haiti. They brought their traditional religions with them, and these religions influenced each other. As missionaries tried to convert the slaves to Roman Catholicism, the Christian religion became mixed in there as well. Over time, these religions mixed together and formed Vodou (the preferred spelling in that country).

For four hundred years, the religion spread to various parts of the world and gained mixed receptions as it traveled. In modern media,

Vodun (often called Voodoo) is both demonized and sensationalized, but in many parts of West Africa, it's an intricate system of spirituality that touches on matters like justice and philosophy. At its roots, Vodun is an animism religion, and worshipers believe that everything has vodou, or spirit. The religion has many different deities, and people worship differently according to their location. Vodun gods can be merciful, petty, cruel, and kind. They have human traits and require sacrifices from the faithful.

Vodun religious ceremonies and festivals are usually joyous occasions and aim to bring hope to people. For example, in Togo, the people observe the Epe-Ekpe Festival, which celebrates the new year for the Guin people and usually takes place in September. This celebration brings families together. Another ceremony involves the god Sakpata, who causes rain and smallpox. Women dance in bright dresses with colorful patterns to appease the god. While the religion used to include human sacrifices, priests only sacrifice animals now.

Vodou traditional drum

Thom Quine, CC BY-SA 2.0 <https://creativecommons.org/licenses/by-sa/2.0>, via Wikimedia Commons
https://commons.wikimedia.org/wiki/File:Antique_Haitian_Vodou_ceremonial_drum.jpg

The religion is incredibly intricate, with various traditions and rites that are guarded by the priestly class. The people worship their ancestors and use talismans in their worship. However, Vodun also includes spells and taboos that are seen as "evil." Vodun has become an integral part of West African culture and has a massive following in various parts of the region.

There are many cultures in West Africa with their own unique traditions and beliefs. Despite the various upheavals that the region experienced in its history, these cultures remained steadfast and survived, while other cultures disappeared and went extinct. West Africa is a melting pot of languages, cultures, and heritages that make it one of the most intriguing regions in the world.

Conclusion

West Africa is made up of sixteen countries that each had to fight for their independence and have their own unique mix of cultures, languages, and traditions. Many of those countries share common ancestors and beliefs, which show that there was a time when the region had different borders that existed naturally. Despite all the difficulties the region has faced, it has maintained a unique and colorful personality.

From the beginning of history, the region has had interesting cultures that traveled extensively and set up the incredible trans-Saharan trading system. Soon, the nomadic people began to farm fertile lands and discovered how to work with metal. The remains of the prehistoric communities at Dhar Tichitt and its surroundings show how the ancient West Africans interacted with their environment. They managed to overcome hostile weather patterns, wild animals, and the challenges of building an established society. For hundreds of years, they thrived and built an intricate culture. In time, they moved on to Djenné-Djenno and learned how to create urban civilizations. Some of the ancient cities still remain, and despite a mysterious past, they're still flourishing with a modern population. For instance, the city of Ile-Ife stood through turbulent times and boasts a rich and storied history.

In time, small urban settlements turned into mighty kingdoms that eventually made up the golden empires that thrived during the Middle Ages. The empires of Ghana and Mali were wealthy beyond belief and controlled some of the most profitable trade routes and cities in the world. Their legacy was so incredible that for centuries after their collapse, people were still talking about their riches and status. Meanwhile, the Songhai Empire proved that West Africa could sustain an empire without the gold mines that made Ghana and Mali rich. These empires were incredibly powerful and had an indelible impact on West Africa's history. When the Gold Coast gained its independence, the people chose the name of Ghana, the historic empire that brought justice and prosperity to its inhabitants.

When West African empires collapsed, and the region entered its darkest history, the people showed their resilience and strength by fighting back against incredible odds and injustice. While the slave trade ripped through the region, some West Africans became rich and supplied slaves. Others had their homes and identities stolen from them. The slave castles and barracoons that remain tell about the brutality of the slave trade, while the cultures that survived are a testament to the endurance of humanity. Modern governments go to great lengths to ensure that the voices of the slaves who left through the "Doors of No Return" will never be silenced.

And while West Africa's troubles didn't end once the slave trade died down, many West Africans never stopped fighting against colonialization. They worked on plantations, endured under colonial governments, and fought in two world wars that otherwise wouldn't have involved them. And once the world emerged from the horrors of World War II, West Africa rose up against colonialization and didn't stop fighting until its nations were free.

From the beginning to modern times, West Africa has been a fascinating region that is well worth studying.

Here's another book by Captivating History that you might like

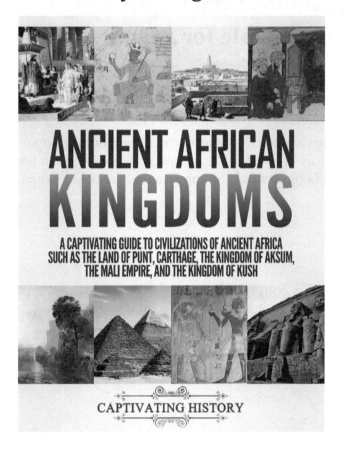

Free Bonus from Captivating History (Available for a Limited time)

Hi History Lovers!

Now you have a chance to join our exclusive history list so you can get your first history ebook for free as well as discounts and a potential to get more history books for free! Simply visit the link below to join.

Captivatinghistory.com/ebook

Also, make sure to follow us on Facebook, Twitter and Youtube by searching for Captivating History.

References

"Yoruba Religion." https://en.m.wikipedia.org/wiki/Yoruba_religion

"Yoruba Folk Tales." https://yorubafolktales.wordpress.com

"Oduduwa." https://en.m.wikipedia.org/wiki/Oduduwa

Sheriff, Oshin. "Sango, the Yoruba God of Thunder and Lightning." March 2018. https://medium.com/@OGBENISKILLA/sango-the-yoruba-god-of-thunder-and-lightning-99e8111c10d2

"Ogun." https://en.m.wikipedia.org/wiki/Ogun

"Oshun." https://en.m.wikipedia.org/wiki/Oshun

Akintoye, Stephen Adebanji. *A History of the Yoruba People*. 2010.

Ogundiran, Akinwumi. *The Yoruba: A New History*. November 2020.

Johnson, Samuel. *The History of the Yorubas from the Earliest Times to the Beginning of the British Protectorate*. First published 1921.

Link: https://www.britannica.com/place/western-Africa

Date Accessed: 10/01/22

Title: western Africa

Link: https://wasscehistorytextbook.com/12-the-environment-in-west-african-history/

Date Accessed: 10/01/22

Title: The Environment in West African History

Link: https://www.jstor.org/stable/523423

Date Accessed: 10/01/22

Title: Land Use Change in the Harsh Lands of West Africa

Link: https://www.metmuseum.org/toah/hd/gold/hd_gold.htm

Date Accessed: 13/01/22

Title: The Trans-Saharan Gold Trade (7ᵗʰ -14ᵗʰ Century)

Link: https://www.thoughtco.com/trade-across-the-sahara-44245

Date Accessed: 13/01/22

Title: Trade Across the Sahara

Link: https://www.worldhistory.org/article/1342/the-salt-trade-of-ancient-west-africa/

Date Accessed: 13/01/22

Title: The Salt Trade of Ancient West Africa

Link: https://wasscehistorytextbook.com/3-islam-in-west-africa-introduction-spread-and-effects/#:~:text=Islam%20promoted%20trade%20between%20West,settled%20in%20the%20commercial%20centres.

Date Accessed: 13/01/22

Title: Islam in West Africa. Introduction, spread and effects

Link: https://www.worldhistory.org/article/1382/the-spread-of-islam-in-ancient-africa/

Date Accessed: 13/01/22

Title: The Spread of Islam in Ancient Africa

Link:
https://spice.fsi.stanford.edu/docs/the_spread_of_islam_in_west_africa_containm
ent_mixing_and_reform_from_the_eighth_to_the_twentieth_century

Date Accessed: 13/01/22

Title: The Spread of Islam in West Africa: Containment, Mixing, And Reform
from Eighth to the Twentieth Century

Link: https://www.jstor.org/stable/29737901?seq=1#metadata_info_tab_contents

Date Accessed: 13/01/22

Title: Islam as a Factor in West African Culture

Link: https://www.britannica.com/place/western-Africa/The-beginnings-of-
European-activity

Date Accessed: 14/01/22

Title: The beginnings of European Activity

Link: https://www.khanacademy.org/humanities/art-africa/african-art-
introduction/african-art-europe/a/african-art-effects-of-european-colonization

Date Accessed: 14/01/22

Title: African art and the effects of European contact and colonization

Link: https://www.jstor.org/stable/45197784

Date Accessed: 14/01/22

Title: Western Influences and Activities in Africa

Link: https://www.ushistory.org/us/6a.asp

Date Accessed: 14/01/22

Title: Western Africa Society at the Point of European Contact

Link: https://www.historytoday.com/archive/west-africa-prehistory

Date Accessed: 14/01/22

Title: West Africa in Prehistory

Link: https://www.jstor.org/stable/27850711

Date Accessed: 14/01/22

Title: West African Prehistory: Archaeological studies in recent decades have illuminated the prehistory of this vast region, revealing unexpected complexity in its development from 10,000 B.C. to A.D. 1000

Link: https://www.britannica.com/topic/Mande

Date Accessed: 14/01/22

Title: Mande

Link: https://ui.adsabs.harvard.edu/abs/2009CRGeo.341..703H/abstract

Date Accessed: 14/01/22

Title: Coping with uncertainty: Neolithic life in the Dhar-Tichitt-Walata, Mauritania (ca 4000-2300 BP)

Link: https://www.cambridge.org/core/books/abs/cambridge-world-history/tichitt-tradition-in-the-west-african-sahel/FA8A6F2725008517F6ABD93007B96405#access-block

Date Accessed: 14/01/22

Title: The Tichitt tradition in the West African Sahel

Link: https://www.researchgate.net/publication/334154351_The_Emergence_of_Mobile_Pastoral_Elites_during_the_Middle_to_Late_Holocene_in_the_Sahara

Date Accessed: 14/01/22

Title: The Emergence of Mobile Pastoral Elites during the Middle to Late Holocene in the Sahara

Link: http://www.homepages.ucl.ac.uk/~tcrndfu/articles/McDonaldVernetFullerWoodhouse.pdf

Date Accessed: 17/01/22

Title: New Light on the Tichitt Tradition: A preliminary report on survey and excavation at Dhar Nema

Link: https://www.researchgate.net/publication/232873688_Dhar_Nema_From_early_agriculture_to_metallurgy_in_southeastern_Mauritania

Date Accessed: 17/01/22

Title: Dhar Néma: From early agriculture to metallurgy in southeastern Mauritania

Link: https://www.worldhistory.org/Djenne-Djenno/

Date Accessed: 17/01/22

Title: Djenne-Djenno

Link: https://whc.unesco.org/en/list/116/

Date Accessed: 17/01/22

Title: Old Towns of Djenné

Link: https://www.britannica.com/place/Ile-Ife

Date Accessed: 17/01/22

Title: Ile-Ife

Link: https://www.blackpast.org/global-african-history/ile-ife-ca-500-b-c-e/#:~:text=Ile%20Ife%2C%20also%20known%20as,estimated%20population%20of%20501%2C000%20people.

Date Accessed: 17/01/22

Title: Ile Ife, Nigeria (CA. 500 B.C.E.-)

Link: https://www.worldhistory.org/Ife/

Date Accessed: 17/01/22

Title: Ife

Link: https://theculturetrip.com/africa/nigeria/articles/the-kingdom-of-ife-nigerias-ancient-city-of-art/

Date Accessed: 17/01/22

Title: The Kingdom of Ife: Nigeria's Ancient City of Art

Link: https://www.thoughtco.com/ile-ife-nigeria-169686

Date Accessed: 17/01/22

Title: Ile Ife (Nigeria)

Link:
https://www.ducksters.com/history/africa/empire_of_ancient_ghana.php#:~:text=Ancient%20Ghana%20ruled%20from%20around,lands%20as%20they%20saw%20fit.

Date Accessed: 21/01/22

Title: Ancient Africa: Empire of Ancient Ghana

Link: https://www.britannica.com/place/Ghana-historical-West-African-empire

Date Accessed: 21/01/22

Title: Ghana

Link: https://www.worldhistory.org/Ghana_Empire/

Date Accessed: 21/01/22

Title: Ghana Empire

Link: https://courses.lumenlearning.com/suny-hccc-worldcivilization/chapter/the-ghana-empire/

Date Accessed: 21/01/22

Title: The Ghana Empire

Link:
https://books.google.co.za/books?id=mP2KSOvJHbMC&pg=PA25&redir_esc=y#v=onepage&q&f=false

Date Accessed: 21/01/22

Title: Empires of Medieval West Africa: Ghana, Mali, and Songhay

Link: https://www.nationalgeographic.org/encyclopedia/mali-empire/

Date Accessed: 22/01/22

Title: The Mali Empire

Link: https://www.britannica.com/place/Mali-historical-empire-Africa

Date Accessed: 22/01/22

Title: Mali

Link: https://www.worldhistory.org/Mali_Empire/

Date Accessed: 22/01/22

Title: Mali Empire

Link: https://courses.lumenlearning.com/suny-hccc-worldcivilization/chapter/mali/

Date Accessed: 22/01/22

Title: Mali

Link: https://oxfordre.com/africanhistory/view/10.1093/acrefore/9780190277734.001.0001/acrefore-9780190277734-e-266

Date Accessed: 22/01/22

Title: The Empire of Mali

Link: https://www.britannica.com/place/Songhai-empire

Date Accessed: 23/01/22

Title: Songhai Empire

Link: https://www.sahistory.org.za/article/songhai-african-empire-15-16th-century

Date Accessed: 23/01/22

Title: Songhai, African Empire, 15th-16th Century

Link: https://www.blackpast.org/global-african-history/songhai-empire-ca-1375-1591/

Date Accessed: 23/01/22

Title: Songhai Empire (CA. 1375-1591)

Link: https://www.worldhistory.org/Songhai_Empire/

Date Accessed: 23/01/22

Title: Songhai Empire

Link: https://courses.lumenlearning.com/suny-hccc-worldcivilization/chapter/songhai/

Date Accessed: 23/01/22

Title: Songhai

Link: https://www.thoughtco.com/biography-sonni-ali-44234

Date Accessed: 24/01/22

Title: Biography of Sonni Ali, Songhai Monarch

Link: https://www.britannica.com/biography/Muhammad-I-Askia

Date Accessed: 24/01/22

Title: Muhammad I Askia

Link: https://www.britannica.com/topic/transatlantic-slave-trade

Date Accessed: 24/01/22

Title: Transatlantic slave trade

Link: https://ldhi.library.cofc.edu/exhibits/show/africanpassageslowcountryadapt/introductionatlanticworld/trans_atlantic_slave_trade

Date Accessed: 24/01/22

Title: The Trans-Atlantic Slave Trade

Link: https://www.metmuseum.org/toah/hd/slav/hd_slav.htm

Date Accessed: 24/01/22

Title: The Transatlantic Slave Trade

Link: https://www.persee.fr/doc/outre_0300-9513_1975_num_62_226_1831

Date Accessed: 24/01/22

Title: Effects of the Atlantic Slave Trade on Some West African Societies

Link: https://www.britannica.com/place/Goree-Island

Date Accessed: 25/01/22

Title: Gorée Island

Link: https://theculturetrip.com/africa/nigeria/articles/how-nigeria-is-preseving-the-legacy-of-its-slave-ports/

Date Accessed: 25/01/22

Title: How Nigeria is Preserving the Legacy of its Slave Ports

Link: https://edition.cnn.com/2018/07/27/africa/ghana-elmina-castle/index.html

Date Accessed: 25/01/22

Title: Inside Ghana's Elmina Castle is a haunting reminder of its grim past

Link:
https://www.ushistory.org/us/27b.asp#:~:text=Life%20on%20the%20fields%20me
ant,overseer%20was%20oftentimes%20the%20worst.

Date Accessed: 25/01/22

Title: Slave Life and Slave Codes

Link:
https://www.joh.cam.ac.uk/library/library_exhibitions/schoolresources/exploratio
n/scramble_for_africa

Date Accessed: 25/01/22

Title: The Scramble for Africa

Link: https://kids.britannica.com/kids/article/Scramble-for-
Africa/632997#:~:text=The%20Scramble%20for%20Africa%20is,power%20were
%20Liberia%20and%20Ethiopia.

Date Accessed: 25/01/22

Title: Scramble for Africa

Link: https://www.thoughtco.com/what-caused-the-scramble-for-africa-43730

Date Accessed: 25/01/22

Title: Events Leading to the Scramble for Africa

Link: https://www.newworldencyclopedia.org/entry/Scramble_for_Africa

Date Accessed: 25/01/22

Title: Scramble for Africa

Link: https://www.britannica.com/place/French-West-Africa

Date Accessed: 25/01/22

Title: French West Africa

Link: https://www.britannica.com/place/British-West-Africa

Date Accessed: 25/01/22

Title: British West Africa

Link: https://www.britannica.com/place/western-Africa/Decolonization-and-the-regaining-of-independence

Date Accessed: 26/01/22

Title: Decolonization and the regaining of independence

Link: https://www.thoughtco.com/chronological-list-of-african-independence-4070467

Date Accessed: 26/01/22

Title: Chronological List of African Independence

Link: https://scholarworks.bgsu.edu/cgi/viewcontent.cgi?article=1048&context=africana_studies_conf

Date Accessed: 26/01/22

Title: The Impact of the Second Word War on the Decolonization of Africa

Link: https://www.un.org/africarenewal/magazine/august-2010/visions-independence-then-and-now

Date Accessed: 26/01/22

Title: Visions of independence, then and now

Link: https://www.britannica.com/topic/Trusteeship-Council

Date Accessed: 26/01/22

Title: Trusteeship Council

Link: https://www.britannica.com/place/Liberia

Date Accessed: 28/01/22

Title: Liberia

Link: https://www.ascleiden.nl/content/webdossiers/african-leaders-independence

Date Accessed: 28/01/22

Title: African leaders of independence

Link: https://www.britannica.com/place/Ghana/Independence

Date Accessed: 28/01/22

Title: Independence of Ghana

Link: https://www.britannica.com/place/Guinea/Independence

Date Accessed: 28/01/22

Title: Independence of Guinea

Link: https://www.culturesofwestafrica.com/category/culture/

Date Accessed: 28/01/22

Title: Cultures of West Africa

Link: https://www.britannica.com/topic/Edo-people

Date Accessed: 28/01/22

Title: Edo

Link: https://www.britannica.com/topic/Akan

Date Accessed: 28/01/22

Title: Akan

Link: https://www.britannica.com/topic/Yoruba

Date Accessed: 28/01/22

Title: Yoruba

Link: https://www.everyculture.com/wc/Mauritania-to-Nigeria/Yoruba.html

Date Accessed: 28/01/22

Title: Yoruba

Link: https://www.jstor.org/stable/1161318#

Date Accessed: 28/01/22

Title: Toward a New Understanding of Akan Origins

Link: https://www.britannica.com/topic/Serer

Date Accessed: 28/01/22

Title: Serer

Link: https://www.everyculture.com/Sa-Th/Senegal.html

Date Accessed: 28/01/22

Title: Senegal

Link: https://www.britannica.com/topic/Igbo

Date Accessed: 28/01/22

Title: Igbo

Link: https://theculturetrip.com/africa/nigeria/articles/an-introduction-to-nigerias-igbo-people/

Date Accessed: 28/01/22

Title: An Introduction to Nigeria's Igbo People

Link: https://www.npr.org/templates/story/story.php?storyId=1666721#:~:text=Vodun%20is%20an%20ancient%20religion,misunderstood%20religions%20on%20the%20globe.

Date Accessed: 28/01/22

Title: Vodun and West Africa's Spiritual Life

Link: https://www.britannica.com/topic/Vodou

Date Accessed: 28/01/22

Title: Vodou

Link: https://www.britannica.com/topic/Wolof

Date Accessed: 28/01/22

Title: Wolof

Link: http://www.scielo.org.za/scielo.php?script=sci_arttext&pid=S1017-04992013000200016

Date Accessed: 28/01/22

Title: The impact of Christianity on sub-Saharan Africa

Link: https://www.everyculture.com/wc/Japan-to-

Mali/Malinke.html#:~:text=The%20majority%20of%20the%20Malinke,and%20d
uring%20outside%20religious%20services.

Date Accessed: 28/01/22

Title: Malinke

Link: https://www.metmuseum.org/toah/hd/tsis/hd_tsis.htm

Date Accessed: 28/01/22

Title: Trade and the Spread of Islam in Africa

Link: https://www.everyculture.com/wc/Rwanda-to-Syria/Wolof.html

Date Accessed: 30/01/22

Title: Wolof

18917660R00146